Quilting
Through the Seasons

Sharon V. Rotz

©2007 Sharon V. Rotz
Published by

krause publications
An Imprint of F+W Publications

700 East State Street • Iola, WI 54990-0001
715-445-2214 • 888-457-2873
www.krausebooks.com

Our toll-free number to place an order or obtain a free catalog is (800) 258-0929.

The following registered trademark terms and companies appear in this publication:
The Warm™ Company; Lite Steam-a-Seam®; Lite Steam-a-Seam 2®; Hobbs Bonded Fibers©;
Hobbs Heirloom 80/20 Premium Batting®; Omnigrid®; Herrschners, Inc©.; Keepsake Quilting©;
Annie's Attic©; Clotilde©, LLC; Connecting Threads©; Superior Threads©; Nancy's Notions©;
Bernina©; Pfaff©; Brother International©; Janome©; Singer©; Baby Lock©; Husqvarna/Viking©;
Home-Sew©, Inc.

Library of Congress Control Number: 2007928197

ISBN 13: 978-0-89689-551-5
ISBN 10: 0-89689-551-3

Designed by Emily Adler and Donna Mummery
Edited by Jean A. Wright

Printed in China

Acknowledgments

I have been blessed with a family who nurtures and supports me, and friends who are a constant source of encouragement. Without them, my life would not be as richly rewarding.

I would like to thank all the people who continuously help and support me, including:

My parents, husband and children, and three special little people: Emily, Bryson, and Nicholas. Life goes on in a marvelous way and all of you keep me on my toes.

The Undercover Quilters, who generously give of their time to help others, and graciously shared their recipes with you.

My family members and friends, who shared their special moments in their lives.

Candy Wiza and Susan Sliwicki, who helped me with the concept for this book.

Jean A. Wright, Donna Mummery, and Emily Adler, for editing and designing this book, and all the Krause Publications' staff who played a part in making this book come to life.

The many quilters who are old friends and new acquaintances, you stretch me out in new directions and constantly teach me.

3

Table of Contents

Table of Contents

Introduction

When is the best time to celebrate? It's today and each new day throughout the changing seasons of the year. Savor the time you share with your family and friends and spice your life with special moments as you linger over treasured memories.

This fine spring day, everything else can wait. The warming sun beckons us. We stretch and unpeel after a long winter nap. We enjoy our walk as we notice new buds and gather the first wildflowers. We return home to save these precious moments in a spring mini quilt.

Summer is here and there is much to do to fill the longer days. We share time with our families celebrating graduations, weddings, anniversaries, and reunions. Our gardens are full of lush and flavorful foods. Our flowers are rich with bright and sun-drenched color. We can bring some of the sun into our homes with lively pillows, piled high, and wall hangings adorned with beautiful golden sunflowers.

As we swing into autumn, we scurry to enjoy the last of the harvest. We cheer for our favorite football team as we snuggle under a comfy throw. As bright leaves fall to the ground and the nights bring cool temperatures, we are ready to relax for a few moments in front of a cozy fire.

The winter snow has fallen throughout the night leaving a pristine blanket across the landscape. We admire the beauty for a moment, then bundle up for a day of play. First we join forces to make a giant snowman. Then it's time for laughing during a friendly snowball fight. Finally, everyone is back in the house for warm drinks and treats. Oh, what a mixture of wooly caps, soggy mittens and wet boots piled high by the door.

Through the magical breezes of spring, the sizzle of summer, the whirlwind of fall afternoons, and the frosty winter mornings, we enjoy it all — Quilting through the Seasons.

I REMEMBER....

In many cultures, history is not written, but spoken from one generation to the next as family members relate stories of times past. Gather your family around the dinner table, and as you pass the food, pass on the family tales. Spend a relaxing evening without the television and unplugged from your favorite music sharing your life experiences.

Talk of the funniest times, the best times, the scariest times, and the saddest times. Grandparents, aunts, uncles, and family friends can tell of childhood adventures. Children will love to hear these stories. My aunt slipped eggs in her beau's pockets and smashed them, ruining his brand new suit. My mom relived the day of the storm that rocked the house and blew the barn away. My dad told everyone that he was going to marry that cute little girl who moved in next door, and on her 18th birthday, he did!

Invite the children to tell their stories as well. You will be totally surprised at what they remember, and how they saw events, not at all as adults recall. You will soon discover that many of the fondest moments are the little things in life.

Whether a large group of young and old, or a quiet conversation between just two, this could be the start of your family's journal that will be remembered for generations to come.

SHARING RECIPES

When families and friends gather, we come with love in our hearts and food in our hands. Because of our strong ties, we share our recipes as easily as we share our life's stories. We return home with lists of ingredients written on the back of envelopes and scraps of paper. Later, we take these directions and alter them to fit our personal tastes and the ingredients of our cupboards. All too soon, the origins of the recipe are lost. (With that in mind, I apologize to those who believe they have not been given proper credit for their culinary delights.)

Through the generosity of a wonderful collection of friends and family, I have been given these recipes, complete with the love and fellowship that comes with them, to share with you.

CHAPTER 1

Breeze into Spring

As the days lengthen and the snow melts away, we eagerly look forward to the first signs of spring. New birds appear at the feeder, and we see a great variety of guests as they stop for a bit on their way northward. The ground is awakening and coming alive as new leaves push their way to the surface through the carpet of dead leaves. The frozen cover of our lakes is slowly disappearing and we are, oh, so anxious.

The warm breezes blow and we feel young and rejuvenated. Cranberry Creek is coming alive with new sounds. Evening brings the song of the spring peepers, our tiny frog friends. We sleep with our window cracked to hear their chorus throughout the night. We feel the breath of spring and our joy abounds as our world is filled with new life.

JOY WALL QUILT
FINISHED SIZE 17½" X 30"

As a child, I remember delightfully picking the first magical flowers of spring and joyfully running home to present them to my mother. Even now, I eagerly search for those first fragile blooms. Capture the magic of the season as you create a "joy"ful wall quilt for your home.

Materials

½ yd. light beige (appliqué background)

Fat quarter multicolored pink/green print (sashing, flowers)

Fat quarter medium/dark green print (border, stems, leaves)

¼ yd. dark green small print (leaves, binding)

⅛ yd. medium/light green print (sashing, J-O-Y)

⅛ yd. medium raspberry print (flowers)

4" x 6" medium raspberry solid (flowers)

⅝ yd. backing

Other Supplies

¾ yd. paper-backed fusible web

Decorative threads for appliqué

Tear-away stabilizer

20" x 32" cotton batting

Invisible or coordinating threads for quilting

Basic sewing tools and supplies

Cut

*Attach fusible web prior to cutting.

- **Light Beige**
  4 rectangles, 5½" x 17½" (appliqué background)

- **Multicolored Pink/Green Print**
  3 rectangles, 2¼" x 17½" (sashing)
  3 Flower B templates*

- **Medium/Dark Green Print**
  2 rectangles, 3" x 17½" (borders)
  3 Stem templates*
  6 rectangles 1¼" x 4¼" (leaves)

- **Dark Green Print**
  3 strips, 2" x width of fabric (binding)
  6 rectangles 1¼" x 4¼" (leaves)

- **Medium/Light Green Print**
  2 strips, 1" x 17½" (folded trim)
  J-O-Y templates*

- **Medium Raspberry Print**
  3 Flower A templates*

- **Medium Raspberry Solid**
  3 Flower C templates*

Construct

Appliqué

1. Trace Flower A and Flower B templates on the paper side of the fusible web. Rough cut the fusible web ¼" larger than the outside of the template. Cut ¼" inside of the drawn line, leaving a "skeleton" of fusible web. This ½" skeleton will be enough to bind the fabric to the background, yet leave the appliqué flexible.

2. Press the skeletons of fusible web to the wrong side of the fabrics. Trim the outside of the flower to the correct shape.

3. Trace Flower C, Stem, and J-O-Y templates on the paper side of the fusible web. Rough cut the fusible web and press to the wrong side of the fabrics. Trim to the correct shape.

4. Right sides together, stitch the 1¼" x 4¼" medium/dark green rectangles to the dark green rectangles. Press the seams open.

FUSIBLE WEB

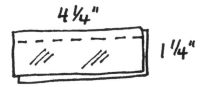

5. Trace the Leaf template on the paper side of the fusible web and rough cut the fusible web. Center the leaf vertically on the seam line and press to the wrong side of the rectangles. Trim to shape.

CENTER ON SEAM

6. Remove paper from the fusible web. Position the appliqué pieces on the background and press to adhere.

7. Pin stabilizer behind the appliqué areas and stitch around the flowers, stems, leaves and letters using a blanket stitch (2.5 length and 2.0 width). For the stems, use a straight stitch close to both edges. Pull threads to the back and tie. Remove stabilizer.

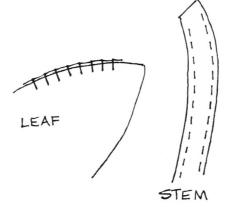

LEAF

STEM

Practice Squares

Practice your decorative stitching on 6" squares of muslin. Write your machine settings, foot used, thread type, and any other helpful information on the muslin with a permanent marker. Keep the squares in a folder for future reference.

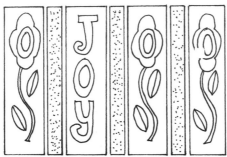

Assemble

1. Lay out the appliquéd sections alternating with the 2¼" multi-colored pink/green print sashing strips. With the right sides together, stitch the sections together.

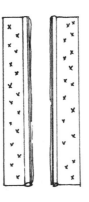

2. With wrong sides together, press the 1" strips of medium/light green in half lengthwise, forming a ½" strip. With raw edges even, baste the folded trim to the right side of one border strip and the left side of the remaining border strip.

3. Lay out the border strips so the folded trim is adjacent to the appliquéd strips. With the right sides together, stitch the borders to the quilt top catching in the folded trim.

Quilt and Bind

1. Layer the quilt top, batting and backing.

2. Echo quilt the appliquéd flowers and letters. Crosshatch the sashing, and quilt horizontal lines in the borders.

3. Piece the 2" binding strips and press lengthwise. Stitch the binding to the quilt. Trim the batting and backing. Turn binding to the quilt back and hand stitch. Refer to The Basics for detailed instructions.

4. Add a label and rod pocket.

TEMPLATES
DRAWN
REVERSED
FOR
FUSING

J-O-Y

J-O-Y

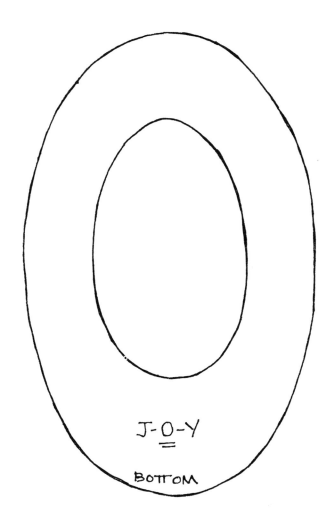

J-O-Y

BOTTOM

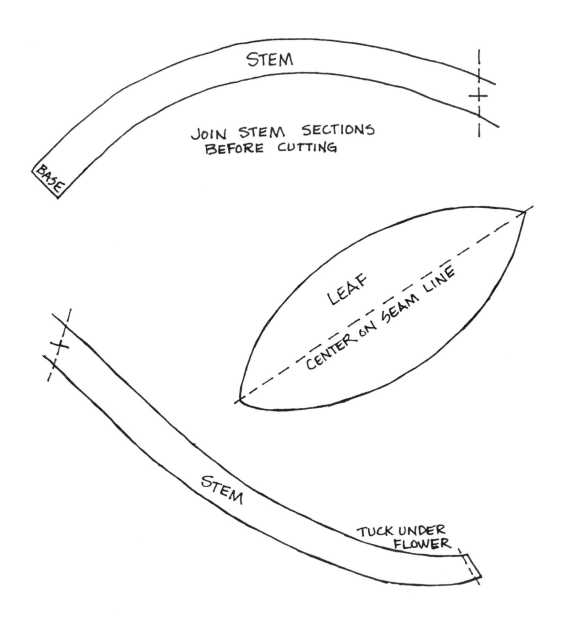

STEM

JOIN STEM SECTIONS
BEFORE CUTTING

BASE

LEAF

CENTER ON SEAM LINE

STEM

TUCK UNDER
FLOWER

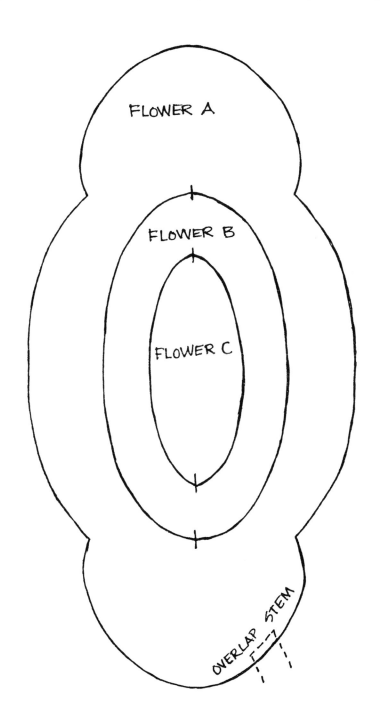

FLOWER A

FLOWER B

FLOWER C

OVERLAP STEM

PUZZLING PULMONARIA ART QUILT
FINISHED SIZE 12" X 12"

With its spotted leaves and pink and blue flowers, is this a flower with an identity crisis, or one that is just trying a bit too hard to please everyone? Commonly known as lungwort, it was thought to relieve wheezing and shortness of breath. It's an eye-catching plant, and you'll enjoy making this three-dimensional art quilt.

Materials

13" x13"" mottled green (background)

Fat quarter med/light green spotted print (leaves)

Fat quarter med/dark green spotted print (leaves)

⅛ yd. dark green (binding)

6" x 6" medium pink/purple (blossoms)

4" x 6" pale blue (blossoms)

13" x 13" backing

Other Supplies

13" x 13" cotton batting

1 yd. paper-backed fusible web

Coordinating thread in pink, blue, and green for quilting

Basic sewing tools and supplies

Cut

*Attach fusible web prior to cutting.

- **Medium/Light Green Print**
  1 Leaf A template for 3-D leaf*
  1 Leaf B template for 3-D leaf*
  1 Leaf B template, reversed*
  2 Leaf C templates*

- **Medium/Dark Green Print**
  1 Leaf A template*
  1 Leaf A template, reversed*
  1 Leaf B, template*

- **Dark Green Print**
  2 strips, 2" x width of fabric (binding)

- **Medium Pink**
  1 Flower A template*
  2 Flower B templates*
  3 Flower C templates*
  2 Flower C templates for 3-D flowers*

- **Pale Blue**
  1 Flower A template*
  1 Flower A template for 3-D flower*
  1 Flower B template*

Construct

Leaves

1. Trace the leaf patterns and reversed leaf patterns on the paper-backed fusible. Rough cut and fuse to the wrong side of the fabrics. Trim to shape.

2. Fuse the 3-D leaves to the wrong side of the remaining med/light green print fabric. Stitch around the edge of the leaves. Trim even with the leaf shape.

3. Fuse the remaining leaves onto the background. (Pale blue flower B is tucked behind the med/dark Leaf B before fusing.) Check the photographs for color placement. The leaves are stitched in place as part of the quilting process.

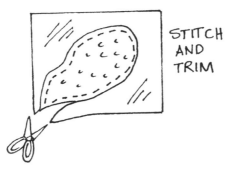

STITCH AND TRIM

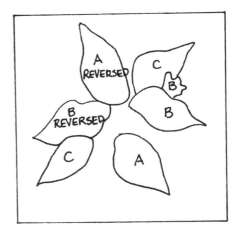

Blossoms

1. Trace the flower patterns on the paper-backed fusible. Rough cut and fuse to the wrong side of the fabrics. Trim to shape.

2. Fuse the 3-D flowers to the wrong side of the corresponding colored fabrics. Stitch the edges of the flowers as you did the leaves. Trim even with the flower shape.

3. Fuse the remaining flowers in place. Check the photographs for color placement. The flowers are stitched as part of the quilting process.

Quilt and Bind

1. Layer the top, batting and backing for quilting. Quilt along the
   edge of the leaves and flowers
   and along the center vein of the
   leaves. Quilt the background
   with echo quilting.

2. Pin the 3-D flowers and leaves
   in place. Quilt along the vein
   lines of the leaves and the
   center or stem ends of the blossoms.

3. Trim quilt to 12" x 12".

4. Piece the 2" binding strips and
   press lengthwise. Stitch the
   binding to the quilt. Trim the
   batting and backing. Turn the
   binding to the back and hand
   stitch. Refer to The Basics for
   detailed instructions.

5. Add a label and rod pocket.

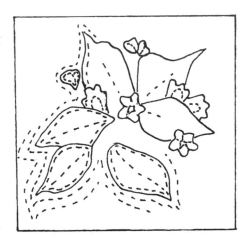

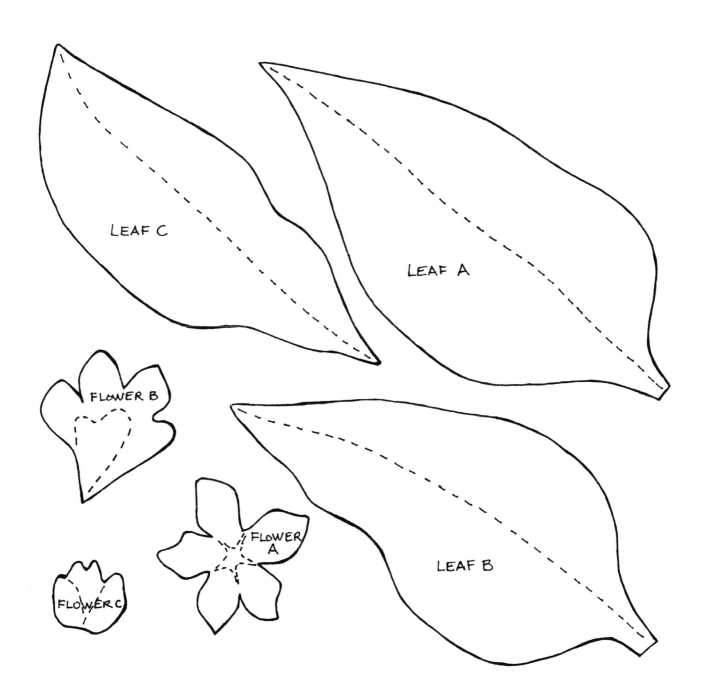

LEAF C

LEAF A

FLOWER B

LEAF B

FLOWER A

FLOWER C

JOY PATCHWORK PILLOW
18" X 18" INCLUDING FLAT RUFFLE

How easy could it be to leap into spring by adding a decorator touch to your room? Pick a handful of your favorite floral fabrics and enjoy bringing some springtime into your home.

Materials

13" x 13" raspberry floral print (pillow center)

5 or 6 coordinating prints, 4½" x 20" (flat ruffle)

½ yd. backing

12" x 12" pillow form

Basic sewing tools & supplies

Cut

- **Raspberry Floral Print**
  1 square 12½" x 12½" (center square)
- **Coordinating Prints**
  20 squares, 3½" x 3½" (coordinating squares)
- **Backing**
  2 rectangles, 13" x 18½"

Adding Dimension

You can add extra dimension to your pillow by quilting the center square prior to pillow top assembly. Choose a lightweight batting.

Construct

1. Lay out the coordinating squares in a random pattern around the center square.

2. Stitch four squares together for each side border of the pillow. Stitch to the center. Press away from the center.

3. Stitch six squares together for the top and bottom borders of the pillow. Stitch to the center. Press away from the center.

4. Using the 13" x 18½" pillow backs, hem one 18½" side by folding 2½" to the wrong side of the fabric. Fold under ½" of the 2½" hem to clean finish the hem edge and machine stitch the hem.

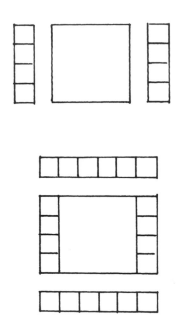

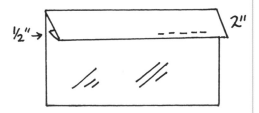

½"→   2"

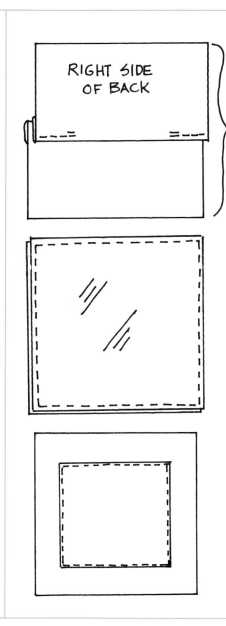

RIGHT SIDE
OF BACK

18½"

5. On the right side of the fabric, overlap the hemmed edges of the pillow backs at the center to measure 18½" x 18½". Pin. Topstitch the overlap 3½" in from the edge on both sides. Backstitch to secure stitching.

6. With right sides together, lay the pillow top on the pillow back and stitch around the outside edge. Turn right side out through the opening in the pillow back. Press.

7. Stitch in the ditch between the patchwork borders and the pillow center to form the flat ruffle edge.

8. Insert the pillow form.

THREE-LETTUCE SALAD

Whether you pick the first harvest from your garden or shop at the local market, a crisp and tasty salad is always a welcome addition to your spring meals. We love the combination of lettuce with fruit and nuts in this salad.

I've used different kinds and combinations of lettuces, and used EITHER grapes OR oranges if I didn't have both on hand. The oranges and grapes more than compensate for the lack of ripe, flavorful tomatoes available in early spring. The toasted almonds are a must in my opinion. They add a nice bit of texture and flavor. I've given this quick and simple recipe out many times, and it's become a favorite among my friends.

Mary Owens
Stevens Point, Wis.

Salad Ingredients

½ bunch butter lettuce, torn into pieces

½ bunch romaine lettuce, torn into pieces

½ bunch leaf lettuce, torn into pieces

1 can mandarin oranges, 11 ounces, drained

1 cup seedless red grapes, cut in pieces

⅓ cup slivered almonds, toasted

1 medium red onion, sliced

Dressing

2 tablespoons olive oil

2 tablespoons red-wine vinegar

1 or 2 cloves garlic, minced

2 teaspoons sugar

Pinch of salt

1. Combine the salad ingredients in a large bowl. Refrigerate.

2. Mix the dressing in a jar, shaking well to dissolve the sugar and salt.

3. Just before serving, pour the dressing over the salad and toss.

Toasting Almonds

Toasting nuts will enhance the flavor. Spread the nuts in a single layer on a cooking sheet. Toast 3 to 5 minutes in a 350-degree oven. Shake the pan once or twice, and watch carefully, they can burn suddenly. Toasting can also be done in a skillet on the stovetop.

Edible Flowers

Edible flowers can add new taste, color and fragrance to your spring salads. Some of the spring flower petals that are edible include: violets, Johnny-Jump-Ups, pansies, dandelions, alliums and chives. Consume only flowers that have been grown specifically for culinary purposes. Flowers from florists, nurseries, garden centers, and even roadsides, may have been treated with pesticides and should not be eaten.

ROSY-RED RHUBARB CAKE

What would spring be without the first-of-the-season rhubarb baked up into something special? My dad called it "pie plant," but today, we are baking up a fabulous cake instead. Thumbs up for this showy and delicious treat.

Rhubarb

The rhubarb plant is a very hardy perennial plant that grows well in both northern and southern climates. The tart stalks are easy to prepare; simply trim, wash, and cook into sauce or your favorite dessert. Generally, the redder the stalks are the sweeter the taste. Rhubarb helps reduce cholesterol, eases digestive problems and contains a generous amount of vitamin C. Do not eat the leaves of rhubarb, the high levels of oxalates are poisonous to many people.

Ingredients

1 yellow cake mix, 18 ounces
4 to 6 cups cut-up rhubarb
1 cup sugar

1 strawberry flavored gelatin, 3 ounces
3 cups miniature marshmallows

1. Preheat oven to 350 degrees.

2. Mix rhubarb and sugar in the bottom of a 9" x 13" pan.

3. Sprinkle with dry gelatin.

4. Cover with marshmallows. Set aside.

5. Prepare cake mix. Pour batter over rhubarb.

6. Bake 45 minutes. (Cake must be fairly dark to be done.)

7. Cool 10 minutes and invert on serving tray.

8. Serve topped with whipped cream.

Lil Chase
Phillips, Wis.

Serving Suggestion

Divide the batter into two 9" round cake pans and bake. Cool 10 minutes. Invert each pan on an elegant glass plate. Serve warm, cut in pie-shaped wedges.

LEMON-FROSTED RASPBERRY COOKIES

Two cooks in the kitchen are sure to sweeten the pot, especially when they are enjoying the fun of making these special cookies. Invite your daughter, granddaughter, or special friend to spend the afternoon making these mouth-watering delights.

Ingredients

1 pound unsalted butter
1 cup sugar
4 egg yolks
2 teaspoons vanilla
½ teaspoon salt

5⅓ cups flour
Raspberry jam (homemade is best)
1 cup sifted powdered sugar
¼ cup fresh lemon juice
   (2 to 3 lemons)

1. Cream butter and sugar until light and fluffy.

2. Add egg yolks one at a time and beat well.

3. Add salt and vanilla.

4. Mix in flour, ½ cup at a time, about 4½ cups.

5. Place dough on a floured board and knead in additional flour.

6. Wrap in plastic and chill for an hour.

7. Preheat the oven to 375 degrees.

8. Roll out dough ¼" thick on a floured board and cut with a 2" round cutter (or a baby food jar).

9. Bake on parchment paper covered cookie sheets 10 to 12 minutes until lightly browned. Cool.

10. Spread half the cookies with raspberry jam and cover with remaining cookies.

11. Mix powered sugar and lemon juice for the frosting. Add only enough lemon juice to make a smooth consistency. Frost cookies.

Elizabeth Vollrath
Stevens Point, Wis.

Cookie Cutters

Get creative with your cookies by trying a variety of cutter shapes. Make a window for the raspberry jam to peek through by using a flower shaped canapé cutter. Cut the extra shape in the cookie tops before baking. Thin the frosting to a glaze consistency and avoid covering the "raspberry window".

"SHAKE DOWN" CRUISE

It began as a small dark spot in the middle of a barren white landscape. By some annual phenomenon, this small, peculiar, dark spot appeared every spring and lit the excitement of a young boy for years to come. You see, this small dark spot in the middle of a frozen Wisconsin lake was the first indication that the spring thaw was coming. This spot, once seen, triggered a yearly ritual that most people would think crazy to perform. For the next several weeks, I would spend my time doing any task imaginable, hopefully bringing us closer to the first voyage of the year known as the "Shake-Down" Cruise.

As the ice began to soften, I found it necessary to crawl onto that frozen landscape and hunt for dark air pockets, frantically jamming sticks into them, trying to break the cover which had shielded our beloved lake all winter. Mom and Dad said "Stay off the lake," but there I was running up the hill, tears flowing, clutching a wet boot and dirty sock. Obviously, I should have heeded their warning.

As the ice loosened its grip on "MY" lake, it was out with the Coast Guard approved ice-breaking boat — our little yellow canoe. Full speed ahead! Boom! Crack! Slowly the yellow cutter made its way towards the far reaches of the lake, through ice that was hungry to take a bite of the canoe's fragile hull. Finally, a clear path was formed, satisfying the requirements Dad had spelled out weeks earlier, "As soon as we have a clear path from the landing to the dock, we will go on our annual voyage." Oh, what a wonderful voyage that would be!

The snow was melting and dripping on the asphalt driveway as we pulled the newly-waxed boat out of the garage. Both Dad and I smiled, so proud of our boat and how it sparkled in the early April sun. With chests puffed out, and bundled in jackets three inches thick, we drove down to the gas station to "Fill 'er Up" and on to the boat landing. Driving past empty parking spots, we knew all too soon the road would be packed with summertime vacationers.

When Dad backed the boat into the water for the first time each year, we had no idea what to expect. With a turn of the key and the spit and sputter of the motor, we turned into adventurers for the day. If Mother Nature gave us 40 degrees and rain; we gladly took it with a smile. Nothing feels quite like cold rain on the cheeks as you bounce effortlessly across a vast empty lake, all the while sporting a gigantic, frozen, toothy grin on your face.

If we forgot to put the plug in the boat, we had a plan to plug the hole by whatever means necessary, no matter how many fingers turned blue. No matter what might happen on the Shake Down Cruise, it was the best boat ride of the year — a truly special time for our family. This would be the first of many summer rides and one we looked forward to from the moment the blue tarp was stretched over our vessel late last October.

Jeff Rotz
Flowery Branch, Ga.

CHAPTER 2

Sizzle into Summer

The days have lengthened, and under a canopy of leaves, we enjoy the long, hot days of summer. On Cranberry Creek, the peepers have been replaced by the twang of the green frogs and the deep call of the bull frogs. The mallard hen cruises the shallows with her new brood and the lily pads are showing their heads above the waterline.

We turn to the outdoors as we entertain our family and friends. Vacations, picnics, family gatherings and plenty of water and sun fill each day. This is the season to bask in the sunshine, and we rise early and play late to capture each moment. Our gardens are alive with an abundance of colorful blooms and we can't resist bringing the brilliance inside with our cheery sunflower pillows.

SUNFLOWER PILLOW
FINISHED SIZE: 24" INCLUDING PETALS

Growing sunflowers in the house? Your guests will do a double take when they see this giant sunflower pillow.

Materials

1 yd. mottled golden yellow (petals)
Fat quarter sunflower print (center)
Fat quarter coordinated backing
2 yd. paper-backed fusible web (18" wide)
½ yd. muslin (underlining)
12" round pillow form
Basic sewing tools and supplies

Cut

- **Mottled Golden Yellow**
  20 petals* (attach fusible web prior to cutting)
  Use remainder for backs of petals
- **Sunflower Print**
  13" circle
- **Backing**
  13" circle
- **Muslin**
  Two 13" circles

Construct

1. Cut the mottled golden yellow into ½ yard pieces. Press fusible web to the wrong side of one piece of the fabric. (Press fusible web to the wrong side of both half-yard pieces for extra firm petals.) Remove paper. Trace 20 petals onto the wrong side of one fusible-web-covered yellow fabric. Leave room between the petals for seam allowances.

FUSIBLE WEB ATTACHED

Trimming Seams

Trim seams with pinking shears or notch seam allowances to remove some of the bulk on curved edges.

2. With the right sides together, match the fusible-covered fabric with the second piece of fabric. Stitch around each petal on the drawn line, leaving the bottom edge open. Backstitch at the beginning and end of the seam.

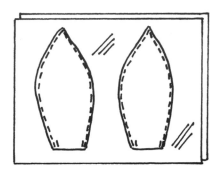

3. Turn to the right side. Press. Make a small pleat in the bottom edge, and baste in place.

4. Pin the muslin underlining to the wrong side of the pillow front and pillow back.

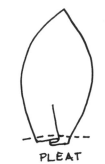

PLEAT

5. Arrange the petals around the pillow front and baste in place, catching in the muslin underlining.

6. Right sides together, stitch the pillow top to the pillow back with a ½" seam. Leave a 9" to 10" opening for turning.

7. Insert pillow form. Neatly stitch opening closed.

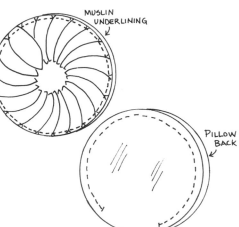

MUSLIN UNDERLINING

PILLOW BACK

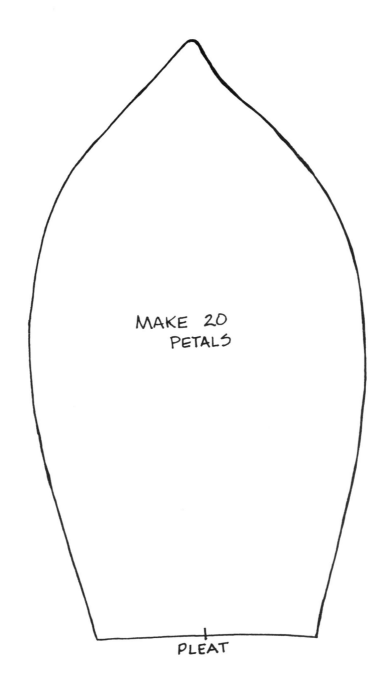

MAKE 20
PETALS

PLEAT

SUNFLOWER CUBE PILLOWS

SET OF TWO COMPLEMENTARY PILLOWS

FINISHED SIZE: 18" X 18"

Use pillows to freshen your home with a new summer look. With the clean lines and classy look of your Sunflower Cube Pillows, you can pile them high or scatter them around to set a sunny mood indoors.

Materials

Fabric (for 2 complementary pillows)

⅓ yd. sunflower print (pillow top)

⅓ yd. yellow solid (pillow top)

⅓ yd. dark-brown solid (pillow top)

⅝ yd muslin (pillow lining)

⅝ yd. coordinating fabric (pillow backs)

Other Supplies

2 squares cotton batting, 20" x 20"

Two 18" x 18" pillow forms

15" x 15" square ruler

Invisible or coordinating thread (quilting)

Basic sewing tools and supplies

Cut

- **Sunflower Print**
  3 strips, 3½" x width of fabric
- **Yellow Solid**
  3 strips, 3½" x width of fabric
- **Dark-Brown Solid**
  3 strips, 3½" x width of fabric
- **Muslin**
  2 squares, 20" x 20"
- **Pillow Backing**
  2 squares, 20" x 20"

Maximize the Use of Your Fabric

By offsetting the strips before piecing, you may be able to cut four pieces from each set of strips, thus eliminating the need for a third set of strips. Offset the strips by dropping the second strip down 2½" from the first strip and the third strip 2½" from the second strip. Start cutting your triangles close to the ends of the offset strips.

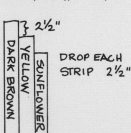

Construct

1. Stitch the strips in the following order. Use the sunflower print as the top strip, yellow as the middle strip, and dark brown as the bottom strip. Make three sets of strips and press seam allowances to one side. From these strips, you will be able to cut the pieces needed for two pillows that have opposite colorings.

2. Using a 15" x 15" ruler, cut 45-degree triangles from the strips. If you set your ruler with zero at the tip of the triangle, the two sides of the triangles should be 13⅜" long. Use masking tape to mark your ruler for easy reference when cutting the remaining triangles.

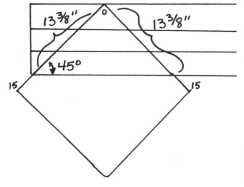

3. Alternate cutting the triangles so the sunflower print is at the tip of triangle 1, the bottom of triangle 2, and the tip of triangle 3. For the second set of strips, start with the sunflower print on the bottom of triangle 1, the tip of triangle 2, and the bottom of triangle 3. Cut the remaining two triangles from the third set of strips.

4. Re-press the seam allowances of two matching triangles toward the sunflower print and the other two matching triangles away from the sunflower print. Do the same for the second pillow top.

5. Lay out the matching triangles in a square, alternating the pressed seam allowances. Sew the adjacent triangles together forming half of the pillow top. Press the seam allowances in opposite directions. Stitch the two halves together to complete the pillow top.

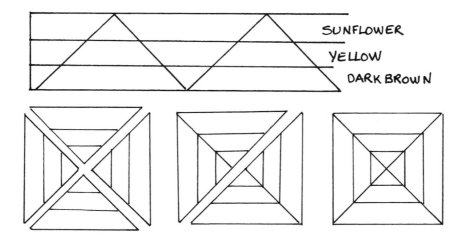

SUNFLOWER

YELLOW

DARK BROWN

6. Layer the pillow top and batting on top of the muslin. Quilt by stitching on the diagonal seam lines and then 1¼" from the previous stitching lines. Trim even with the edges of the pillow top.

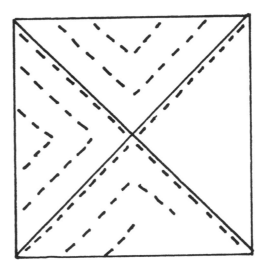

7. Center the quilted pillow top on the pillow backing with right sides together. Stitch around the pillow, rounding off the corners slightly as shown. Leave an opening approximately 9" to 10" long on one side for turning the pillow.

8. After turning the pillow, insert the pillow form and neatly hand stitch the opening closed.

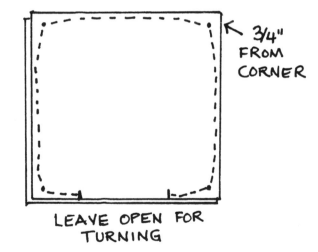

↖ 3/4" FROM CORNER

LEAVE OPEN FOR TURNING

SUNFLOWER CUBE WALL QUILT
FINISHED SIZE 30" X 30"

This wall quilt, full of bold color, graphic design and sparkling sunflowers, has spanned the gap between country classic and city chic. No matter what your style is, add a sunny disposition to your home.

Materials

⅞ yd sunflower print (blocks, binding)

¾ yd. dark brown solid (blocks)

⅓ yd yellow solid (blocks)

1 yd. backing

32" x 32" cotton batting

Invisible or coordinating thread (quilting)

12" x 12" square ruler

Basic sewing tools and supplies

Cut

- **Sunflower Print**
  6 strips, 2" x width of fabric (border blocks)
  4 strips, 2" x width of fabric (binding)
  3 strips, 2" x width of fabric (center blocks)

- **Dark Brown Solid**
  8 strips, 2" x width of fabric (border blocks)
  3 strips, 2" x width of fabric (center blocks)

- **Yellow Solid**
  2 strips, 2" x width of fabric (border blocks)
  3 strips, 2" x width of fabric (center blocks)

Edge Guide

Use a ¼" machine foot with an edge guide, or place a piece of foam tape on the machine ¼" from the needle to guide your fabrics when stitching strips. Position the tape along or in front of the machine foot. Be careful not to place the tape on the feed dogs.

Construct

Center Blocks

1. Stitch the center strips together in the following order. Use the sunflower print as the top strip, the yellow as the middle strip and the dark brown as the bottom strip. Make three sets of strips. Press seam allowances to one side.

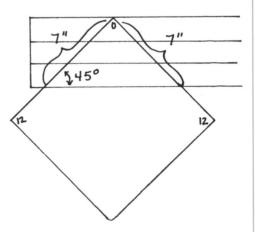

2. Using a 12" x 12" ruler, cut 45-degree triangles from the strips. If you set your ruler with zero at the tip of the triangle, the two sides of the triangles should be 7" long. Use masking tape to mark your ruler for easy reference when cutting the remaining triangles.

3. Alternate cutting the triangles so the sunflower print is at the tip of triangle 1, the bottom of triangle 2, and the tip of triangle 3, etc. On the second set of strips, start with the sunflower print on the bottom of triangle 1, the tip of triangle 2, and the bottom of triangle 3. Cut any remaining triangles needed from third sets of strips.

4. Re-press the seam allowances of two matching triangles toward the sunflower print and the other two matching triangles away from the sunflower print. Lay out the triangles in a square, alternating the seam allowances.

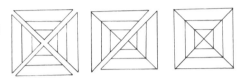

5. Sew the adjacent triangles together. Press the seam allowances in opposite directions. Stitch the two halves together to complete the block. Make two blocks with the sunflower print on the outside of the block and two blocks with the dark brown on the outside of the block.

6. Alternating blocks, lay out as a four patch and stitch together.

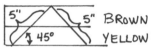

5" 5" BROWN
45° YELLOW

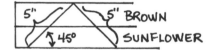

5" 5" BROWN
45° SUNFLOWER

Border Blocks

1. Stitch two dark brown strips to two yellow strips. Press seam allowances to one side.

2. Using a 12" x 12" or smaller square ruler, cut 45-degree triangles as you did for the center blocks. The sides of these blocks will be 5". Re-press the seam allowances and stitch into two blocks with the dark brown on the outside of the block and two blocks with the yellow on the outside of the block.

3. Stitch six dark brown strips to six sunflower print strips. Press seam allowances to one side.

4. Using a 12" x 12" or smaller square ruler, cut 45-degree triangles. Again, the sides will measure 5". Re-press the seam allowances and stitch into six blocks with the dark brown on the outside of the block and six blocks with the sunflower print on the outside of the block.

Quilt and Bind

1. Lay out the quilt top as shown. Stitch the side blocks together and sew to the sides of the quilt top. Stitch the top and bottom blocks together and sew to the quilt top.

2. Layer the quilt top, batting and backing. Quilt squares in all of the blocks.

3. Piece the remaining four sunflower print strips for the binding and press lengthwise.

4. Stitch the binding to the quilt. Trim the batting and backing. Turn binding to the quilt back and hand stitch. Refer to The Basics for additional instruction.

5. Add a rod pocket and label.

CHINESE CHICKEN SALAD

Main-dish salads are a cool and flavorful meal on hot summer days. Prepare the ingredients ahead, refrigerate, and toss the salad just before serving.

Ingredients

1½ pounds skinless, boneless chicken breasts

Marinade

4 tablespoons soy sauce

1 tablespoon dark sesame oil

Salad

1 large head Napa cabbage, ends trimmed and sliced thin

6 green onions, sliced thin

3 tablespoons butter

1 package chicken ramen noodles, crushed

½ cup sliced almonds

½ cup sunflower seeds

Dressing

¾ cup corn oil

3 tablespoons apple-cider vinegar

2 tablespoons soy sauce

1 flavor packet from chicken ramen noodles

¼ cup sugar

1. Place the chicken breasts in a heavy self-sealing plastic bag. If the chicken breasts are an uneven thickness, pound gently to even.

2. Whisk together the marinade ingredients. Pour over the chicken. Seal and refrigerate 1 hour or more.

3. Place the sliced cabbage and onions in a large serving bowl. Chill.

4. In a large non-stick skillet, melt the butter over medium heat. Add the crushed noodles and almonds and heat until golden brown, stirring often.

5. Add sunflower seeds to the noodles and almonds. Remove to a paper towel and cool.

6. Combine the dressing ingredients in a blender or whisk by hand until blended. Set aside.

7. Heat a skillet until hot. Sauté the chicken breasts until the juices run clear, about 6 minutes. Cool.

8. Slice the cooled chicken into bite-size pieces.

9. Toss the chicken, cabbage, nut mixture and dressing. Serve immediately.

Linda Schober
Waupaca, Wis.

Sunflower Seeds

Bright yellow sunflowers grow on stalks up to ten feet tall and have long been adored as a symbol of the sun. Aztec sun priestesses were crowned with sunflowers and wore jewelry with sunflower motifs. The seeds are nutrient rich sources of B vitamins, iron and potassium.

RASPBERRY ICED TEA

Hot summer afternoons are the right time for a tall cool drink and we can't resist the refreshment of our favorite iced tea. Have a pitcher full in the refrigerator to share with friends who stop by to visit.

I make ice cubes with a raspberry frozen inside and serve with a slice of lemon. I've also used this recipe as a punch with a fruit filled ice ring. Mix six black and three green tea bags for a slightly different taste.

Karen McDowell
Zephyrhills, Fla.

Ingredients

4 quarts water
¼ cup sugar or artificial sweetener
12 ounces frozen raspberries

9 tea bags
¼ cup lemon juice

1. Bring water to a boil. Remove from heat and stir in sugar until dissolved.

2. Add raspberries, tea bags, and lemon juice. Cover and steep for 3 minutes.

3. Strain; discard berries and tea bags.

4. Serve over ice.

LEMON FLUFF

Summer is the perfect time to gather family and friends. Whether we picnic in the backyard or at the park on the lake, everyone takes part in the fun-filled games. Later, we are eager to fill our plates at a table overflowing with delicious food.

Ingredients

1 can evaporated milk, 14½ ounces
1 package lemon gelatin, 3 ounces
1¾ cups hot water
¼ cup lemon juice

Fresh lemon rind, grated
1 cup sugar
2½ cups vanilla wafer crumbs

1. Chill milk at least 3 to 4 hours.

2. Dissolve gelatin in hot water. Chill until partially set.

3. Whip until light and fluffy adding lemon juice, lemon rind and sugar.

4. Whip chilled milk and fold into gelatin mixture.

5. Line the bottom of a 9"x13" pan with wafer crumbs, reserving about ½ cup crumbs for top.

6. Pour gelatin mixture into crumb-lined pan and top with reserved crumbs.

7. Chill until firm. Cut into squares. Serves 12.

Growing up, we always knew it was a special occasion when my Mom made Lemon Fluff, a recipe handed down to her by my grandmother. For many years, my parents hosted a family reunion picnic and Lemon Fluff was a part of that reunion picnic. It brings back memories of how hot the summers could be and how cool, refreshing and luscious the Lemon Fluff tasted.
Betsy Scuglik
Kenosha, Wis.

Zest It Up

Add the colorful lemon peel for extra lemony goodness. Lemon juice and lemon zest are packed with power to heal cuts and bruises and help prevent breast cancer.

MOTHER'S PEACH KUCHEN

Ah, the luscious fruits of summer so ripe and juicy, we just can't resist them. Combine the delightful taste of peaches and cream in this delicious coffee cake.

My mother would make this in the summer with fresh peaches that she bought by the crate for canning. Throughout the rest of the year, she would use her home-canned peaches.

Ruth Kulas
Stevens Point, Wis.

Baking with fresh peaches

Slice 3 to 4 large peaches. Sprinkle the slices with sugar to draw out the juices. Drain and use the juice in the custard, adding water, if necessary, to make ½ cup.

Ingredients

1½ cups flour
½ teaspoon salt
½ cup butter
1 can sliced peaches, 29 ounces

½ cup sugar
½ teaspoon cinnamon
1 cup evaporated milk
1 egg, slightly beaten

1. Preheat oven to 375 degrees.

2. Put flour, salt and butter in a bowl. Mix with a pastry blender until crumbly.

3. Press mixture firmly onto the bottom and sides of a greased 9" square pan.

4. Drain the peaches well. Reserve ½ cup syrup.

5. Arrange the peach slices on the crust in the pan.

6. Mix the sugar and cinnamon and sprinkle over the peaches.

7. Bake for 20 minutes.

8. Mix the reserved syrup, evaporated milk, and egg. Pour over the peaches.

9. Bake 30 minutes more or until custard is firm.

10. Serve warm or cold.
Serves 9

AT THE COTTAGE

As a child, I remember spending the long summer days at my grandparent's cottage near a lake in central Wisconsin. My grandma would always have chocolate milk to fill my favorite bird-shaped cup. My brother and I would spend hours playing on the huge rock in their front yard. Later in the day, we would walk down the big hill, swatting mosquitoes all the way to the boat landing to skip rocks across the lake. In the evenings, my parents and grandparents always played cards at the dining table. I can still hear my grandpa's big pinky ring hitting the table with a sharp crack every time he played a card.

Now, I have my own family, and I hope my kids will someday treasure their memories of the days we share with my parents at their cottage on the lake.

Stephanie Bowron
Rochester, Minn.

Cinnamon

Cinnamon is one of the oldest spices dating back to 2700 B.C. It was used in perfumes and incense, as well as food and medicine. The bark is stripped off trees and rolled into quills (cinnamon sticks). When the cinnamon is ground, it loses its flavor more rapidly, so buy small amounts and store in a cool, dry place.

CHAPTER 3

Tumble into Autumn

The maples started it by stealing the colors from a summer sunset. The world soon glows in sunny yellows as the birch and aspen reach their peak. Not to be outdone, the majestic oaks fill our eyes with deep reds and mahoganies until the entire skyline is ablaze with color.

Each day the ground is covered with fallen leaves. Neighbors chat as they lean on rakes, and children jump into leaf piles. Soon, everyone ends up throwing leaves into the air and then joins in a back-yard football game. This is a grand time of year with leaves swirling around like golden blessings falling from the sky.

Celebrate the season, knowing the days will soon be shorter and the nights colder. Be ready for the change. Choose soft flannel, cozy fleece and a simple design for a quick-and-easy quilt to make in a weekend.

LEAF MY QUILT ALONE
FLANNEL AND FLEECE QUILT
FINISHED SIZE: 56" X 76"

This is a wonderful, soft, cuddly quilt to keep you warm on those crisp autumn days, whether you're at a football game cheering for the home team or relaxing in front of the fire. It's so fast and easy to make with a flannel front and fleece back (no batting). This quilt is in such demand at our house that I couldn't resist naming it "Leaf My Quilt Alone."

Materials

1 yd. burgundy flannel (flannel 1)

1 yd. green leaf-print flannel (flannel 2)

1 yd. gold-mottled flannel (flannel 3)

¾ yd. rust-print flannel (flannel 4)

¾ yd. green/black-print flannel (flannel 5)

¾ yd tan flannel (background)

2½ yd. fleece

Other Supplies

Thread to match the fleece

2 yd. brown novelty yarn or cord (stems)

Invisible thread or decorative thread for couching

Rotary cutter, ruler and mat

Basic sewing tools and supplies

Sewing Flannel

Working with flannel can be challenging, but tame the shrinkage and stretch by pre-washing and starching the flannel. By the time you are finished with the quilt, the flannel will have softened and the first washing will remove the starch.

Cut

- **Flannel 1 (Burgundy)**
  2 strips, 9½" x width of fabric
  Crosscut into
      8 squares, 9½" x 9½"

  2 strips, 3½" x width of fabric
  Crosscut into
      2 rectangles, 3½" x 9½"
      2 rectangles, 3½" x 6½"
      4 squares, 3½" x 3½"

- **Flannel 2 (Green-Leaf Print)**
  2 strips, 9½" x width of fabric
  Crosscut into
      8 squares, 9½" x 9½"

  2 strips, 3½" x width of fabric
  Crosscut into
      2 rectangles, 3½" x 9½"
      2 rectangles, 3½" x 6½"
      4 squares, 3½" x 3½"

- **Flannel 3 (Gold-Mottled)**
  2 strips, 9½" x width of fabric
  Crosscut into
      8 squares, 9½" x 9½"

  2 strips, 3½" x width of fabric
  Crosscut into
      2 rectangles, 3½" x 9½"
      2 rectangles, 3½" x 6½"
      4 squares, 3½" x 3½"

- **Flannel 4 (Rust Print)**
  2 strips, 9½" x width of fabric
  Crosscut into
      8 squares, 9½" x 9½"

  1 strip, 3½" x width of fabric
  Crosscut into
      1 rectangle, 3½" x 9½"
      1 rectangle, 3½" x 6½"
      2 squares, 3½" x 3½"

- **Flannel 5 (Green/Black Print)**
  2 strips, 9½" x width of fabric
  Crosscut into
      8 squares, 9½" x 9½"

  1 strip, 3½" x width of fabric
  Crosscut into
      1 rectangle, 3½" x 9½"
      1 rectangle, 3½" x 6½"
      2 squares, 3½" x 3½"

- **Background (Tan Flannel)**
  5 strips, 3½" x width of fabric
  Crosscut into
      48 squares, 3½" x 3½"

Leaf Blocks

Construct

1. On the wrong side of 32 background squares, draw a diagonal line from corner to corner. Set aside the remaining 16 squares.

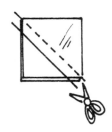

2. With right sides together, match 16 marked background squares with the 16 squares of Flannels 1 to 5. Stitch on the line. Press. Trim away the excess seam allowance corner. Save corners, if desired.

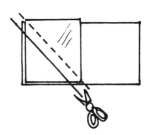

3. With right sides together, align a 3½" marked background square to the lower left corner of the 3½" x 6½" rectangles. Stitch on the line. Press toward the corner. Trim away excess seam allowance.

Marking Tip

Use a sliver of soap to mark lines on dark flannels.

Saving Corners

Save the trimmed corners from the leaf blocks. Stitch them together to make smaller half-square triangles. Trim to a common size and use for another coordinated project.

Couching

Couching is a method of using heavier threads that won't fit through the eye of your sewing machine needle. Trap the threads in place by sewing a zigzag stitch over them using invisible or decorative thread. A couching foot is a helpful accessory available for many sewing machines.

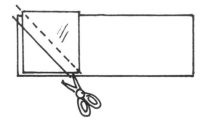

4. With right sides together, align a 3½" marked background square on the lower left corner of the 3½" x 9½" rectangles. Stitch on the line. Press toward the corner. Trim away excess seam allowance.

5. On eight of the remaining background squares, couch a yarn stem diagonally across the block. Using invisible thread, zigzag over two strands of bulky boucle yarn twisted together.

6. Assemble the block as shown.

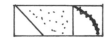

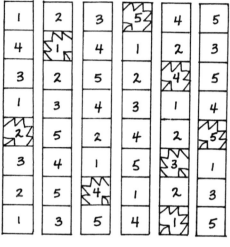

Assemble

1. Lay out the blocks by color as illustrated. Stitch the blocks together in vertical rows. Stitch the vertical rows together completing the quilt top.

2. Carefully fold the fleece in half. Using contrasting thread and a long running stitch, hand baste to mark the vertical center line. Refold the fleece and hand baste to mark the horizontal center line. The fleece is now divided into four quarters.

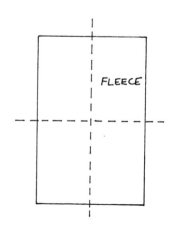

FLEECE

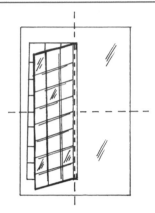 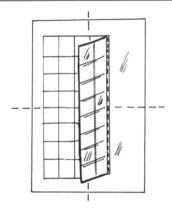

3. Fold the quilt top right sides together exposing the center vertical seam. Use the horizontal basting line to center the quilt top on the fleece. On the wrong side of the fleece, securely pin the center seam allowance of the quilt top to the vertical basting line in the fleece.

4. Using thread to match the fleece, machine stitch in the seam allowance, and attach the top to the fleece. Stitch only through the two layers of the seam allowance and one layer of the fleece. Start and stop at the edge of the quilt top. Backstitch to secure ends.

5. Lay out the quilt again, smoothing the top over the fleece. Fold the quilt top back, exposing the next vertical seam adjacent to the center. Pin securely, again matching the horizontal center seam line of the quilt top to the horizontal basting line of the fleece. Stitch the row in the same manner as the center. Repeat on the other side of center.

6. Repeat the process to secure the two remaining seam allowances. You will have no visible stitching on the top of the quilt. You will have vertical lines stitched on the back (fleece side) of the quilt.

Bind

1. Lay out the quilt. Pin close to, but not on, the outer edges of the quilt top. Trim the fleece to a consistent measurement on the sides of the quilt (approximately 2½").

2. Fold the fleece to the top of the quilt. Tuck under the raw edges of fleece ½", and pin in place catching in the raw edges of the quilt top. You will end up with 1" fleece binding on the quilt sides. Topstitch the sides of the quilt. Use a straight stitch, zigzag, or decorative stitch.

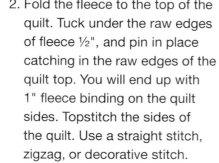

3. Trim the top and bottom of the fleece to a consistent measurement (approximately 5" to 6"). Fold the fleece to the front and tuck under the raw edges of fleece ½". Pin in place. You will have a 2" to 2½" binding on the top and bottom.

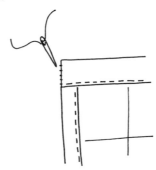

4. Trim away some of the corner bulk. Hand stitch the corners before finishing with machine stitching.

LEAFY PILLOW BANDS

TWO BANDS FOR 18" OR SMALLER PILLOWS

The beauty of fall leaves is so hard to resist that we come in from our afternoon walk with hands full of colorful souvenirs. Certainly they can be used to decorate our home. We used our leaves as patterns to make fun leafy pillow bands that transform our living space into autumn splendor.

Materials

4 yd. black satin ribbon, 1½" wide (pillow bands)

Fat eights of four flannels or assorted flannel scraps (leaf fronts)

½ yd. coordinating flannel (leaf backs)

⅝ yd. black or dark wool felt, 36" wide (leaf batting)

2 yd. paper-backed fusible web

Brown thread (leaf veins)

Collected leaves for patterns

General sewing tools and supplies

Construct

Ribbon Bands

1. Cut the ribbon into two 72" bands. Trim the ends diagonally to prevent raveling.

2. Tie one ribbon around each pillow. Pull snuggly and secure

with a knot. It's much easier to do this before you add the leaves to the bands.

3. Slip the band off the pillow to stitch the leaves to the band.

Family Fun

This is a perfect project to involve the whole family. Everyone can enjoy the outdoors as they search for the perfect leaf to use as a pattern. Younger family members can easily trace the leaves and need not be perfect. You just want the general shape of the leaf. Older family members can handle the cutting, pressing and sewing.

Leaves

1. Following the manufacturer's instructions, adhere ½ yd. fusible web to the wrong side of the ½ yd. coordinating flannel. Remove the paper, and save to use as a pressing sheet in Step 4. Fuse the flannel to one side of the felt.

2. Trace leaf shapes on the paper side of the remaining fusible web. Roughly cut the shapes. Fuse the leaf shapes to the wrong side of the assorted flannels for the leaf fronts.

3. Trim to the correct shape. Remove paper.

4. Make leaf "sandwiches" by placing the trimmed leaves right side up on the felt side of the fabric made in Step 1. (The flannel side will be the backing.) Cover with the reserved paper pressing sheet. Press to fuse the layers together.

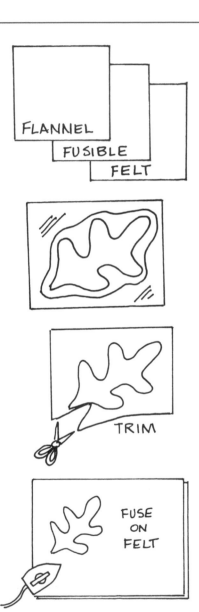

5. Cut off a group of three to four fused leaves. Stitch the leaf veins using brown thread.

6. Trim the individual leaf shapes.

7. Stitch the leaves to the ribbon bands. Slightly overlap the leaves and backstitch to secure. The leaves may be placed only on the ends or completely around the bands.

8. Slide the bands back on the pillows.

Decorating Tip

Add leaves to several lengths of ribbons and use them to decorate your home. Lay them down the center of your dining table over a gold tablecloth or hang them on the edge of your entry mirror.

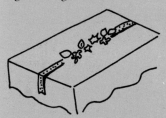

LEAFY COASTER

FINISHED SIZE: 6" X 6"

In the early morning, savor your first cup of coffee or tea as you snuggle into your cozy flannel quilt. Spend a few moments in quiet mediation before the activities of the day, and be the first to greet the sun on frosty mornings.

Materials

7" x 14" burgundy flannel (coaster front and back))

4" x 6" rust-print flannel (leaf)

4" x 6" rust-mottled flannel (leaf)

4" x 6" green leaf-print flannel (leaf)

9" x 12" coordinating flannel (leaf backs)

9" x 12" black or other dark wool felt (leaf batting)

7" x 7" cotton batting (coaster batting)

2 sheets of 9" x 12" paper-backed fusible web

Brown thread (leaf veins)

Smaller, collected leaves for patterns

Basic sewing tools and supplies

Cut and Construct

Coaster

1. From the burgundy flannel, cut two squares 6½" x 6½" (coaster front and back).

2. Place right sides together over the batting. Stitch ¼" from the edges, leaving a 4" opening on one side for turning.

3. Trim the batting as close as possible to the stitching line without cutting the flannel. Turn right side out and press.

4. Turn under the seam allowances of the opening and fuse the opening closed with a scrap of the fusible web.

Leaves

1. Following the manufacturer's instructions, fuse one sheet of fusible web to the wrong side of the coordinating flannel for the leaf backs. Remove the paper and save to use as a pressing sheet for Step 4. Fuse the coordinating flannel to one side of the felt.

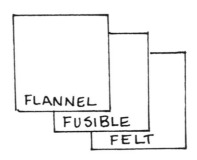

2. Trace three leaf shapes on the paper side of the second sheet of fusible web. Roughly cut the shapes. On the wrong side of the flannels, fuse one leaf shape onto each 4" x 6" flannel.

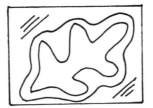

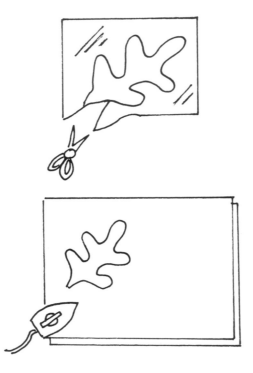

3. Trim to correct shape. Remove the paper.

4. Make a leaf "sandwich" by placing the trimmed leaves right side up on the felt side of the fabric made in Step 1. (The coordinating flannel side will be the backing.) Cover with the reserved paper pressing sheet, and press to fuse the layers together.

5. Using brown thread, stitch leaf veins on your fabric leaves.

6. Trim the individual leaf shapes.

7. Stitch the leaves onto the side edge of the 6" burgundy coaster.

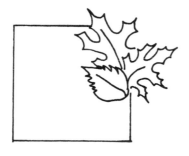

CRANBERRY COCONUT MUFFINS
MAKES 18 MUFFINS

Who can resist the aroma of fresh baked muffins in the morning? Even the grumpiest faces light up as they come to the table. Add a piece of fresh fruit and a glass of milk, and you are well on your way to a bright and healthy day. No one will guess that lurking deep inside these tasty treats are fiber and other nutritional benefits from the flaxseed. Please the palette as well as strengthen the body. What a way to start the day!

Ingredients

2¾ cup all-purpose flour

¼ cup ground flaxseed

½ cup brown sugar

½ cup white sugar

4 teaspoons baking powder

½ teaspoon salt

1 cup coarsely chopped cranberries

½ cup shredded coconut

1 egg, beaten

1½ cups milk

2 tablespoons canola oil

½ teaspoon cinnamon (topping)

2 teaspoons white sugar (topping)

Flaxseed

Flaxseed was used only for animal feed until recently when the health benefits were discovered. It helps to fight breast cancer, control cholesterol and improve kidney function. Flaxseed has a tough, outer shell that cannot be broken down by the body, so it is best to buy cracked or ground flaxseed which can be readily digested. To store, refrigerate or freeze in a tightly sealed container.

1. Preheat the oven to 400 degrees.

2. Mix together flour, flaxseed, brown sugar, ½ cup white sugar, baking powder, and salt in a large bowl.

3. Add cranberries and coconut. Mix together with the dry ingredients to coat them with flour. Make a well in the center of the dry ingredients.

4. Beat together the egg, milk and oil in a separate bowl.

5. Add the milk mixture all at once to the well in the dry ingredients. Stir until just blended. The mixture will look slightly lumpy.

6. Fill greased muffin tins, dividing to make 18 muffins.

7. Mix the cinnamon with 2 teaspoons white sugar. Sprinkle some on top of each muffin before baking.

8. Bake 15 minutes until golden brown.

Baking Tip

For faster preparation time in the morning, measure the dry ingredients into a bowl the night before. Cranberries can also be chopped, refrigerated, and ready to go.

Avoid Over-stirring

Good muffins are slightly rounded on top with no peaks, even in texture, and with no tunnels running from the bottom crust to the top.

RED-LETTUCE SALAD

Apples and cheese are a flavorful combination, and we especially like them tossed together for a fresh taste in a fall salad. Enjoy a visit to your local apple orchard, and pick the best the season has to offer.

Salad Ingredients

1 head red-leaf lettuce
2 red or green apples, chopped
1 cup shredded Swiss or Monterey
   Jack cheese
1 cup cashew nuts

Dressing

½ cup canola oil
½ cup sugar
⅓ cup red-wine vinegar
1 teaspoon grated onion
2 teaspoons poppy seed
1 teaspoon prepared mustard

1. Combine lettuce, apples, cheese, and nuts. Refrigerate.

2. Mix dressing. Pour over salad and toss just before serving.

Kathy Tarcon
Mosinee, Wis.

MINESTRONE SOUP

Warm those chilly bones right down to the toes with piping hot soup. Use the last of the summer harvest to make a mouthwatering feast in a bowl.

Ingredients

1 large onion, chopped
1 pound ground beef
2 cloves of garlic, minced
4 cups beef stock
1 medium eggplant, peeled and diced
3 zucchini 6" to 8" each, diced
3 carrots, diced
2 stalks of celery, diced

8 large tomatoes, peeled and quartered
1 teaspoon salt
1 teaspoon sugar
1 teaspoon oregano
1 teaspoon basil
¼ teaspoon black pepper
½ cup uncooked elbow macaroni

1. Brown the beef and onion. Drain.

2. Place beef and onion in a large kettle with the beef stock.

3. Add the eggplant, zucchini, carrots, celery, tomatoes, salt, sugar, oregano and basil.

4. Simmer 1 to 2 hours.

5. Add the macaroni, and cook 20 minutes longer.

6. If the soup is too thick, add more beef stock until desired consistency.

This is a good hearty soup that makes a lot and freezes well. It's a great way to use all of those surplus garden veggies at the end of the season.
Barb Rogers
Custer, Wis.

Freezing Tip

Freeze extra soup in serving size microwavable containers so it is ready for quick lunches. Leave ½" head space (or more) for expansion.

Fresh Herbs

If substituting fresh basil or oregano for the dry herbs, use 3 to 4 times as much.

Basil

Whether you use it fresh or dried, basil adds a sharp aroma and a spicy flavor to foods. It is especially pleasing when paired with tomatoes. This herb has a reputation for soothing stomach upsets.

Cooking Tip

Tomato peels slip off easily when the tomato is immersed in a pan of boiling water for ½ minute and then placed into cold water.

Nutrition Tip

This soup is an excellent way to pack in the 3 to 5 daily servings of vegetables as recommended by the USDA food pyramid. Vary your choices, and include plenty of dark green and orange vegetables in your diet.

BEER BREAD

Here is a recipe so fast and easy, even a "non-cook" can make it. Try it as a change from the crackers with sausage and cheese snacks.

Ingredients

3 cups self-rising flour
3 tablespoons sugar

1 can of beer, 12 ounces, (room temperature)
3 tablespoons butter, melted

1. Preheat the oven to 350 degrees.

2. Mix the flour, sugar, and beer and pour into a greased loaf pan.

3. Pour melted butter over the top.

4. Bake 50 to 60 minutes.
Makes one loaf

Fran Novak
Stevens Point, Wis.

PLAYING IN THE LEAVES

Autumn is here. The green canopy of leaves that protected us from the scorching summer sun has turned into a colorful display surrounding us in a golden glow. As the leaves fall to the ground, the world opens up and I rustle through the colorful confetti on a trip to the garden.

I think of the many happy autumns we had as our children grew. When the leaves reached a deep mat covering our yard, we got out the tools and started raking them together. The piles grew huge as we worked our way across the back yard. Soon, there was a thick and colorful mattress surrounding the children's play house. Our young explorers climbed up on the low roof, only to leap yelling and giggling, into the flying leaves. Not to be out done, our black lab decided that she, too, needed to be part of the action, and was up on the roof and diving in as well.

It was never an efficient way to clear the yard, but it was a high-spirited and totally fun way to get the job done. The short afternoon soon waned, and we scurried to rake the leaves into the open garden. Then, we hurried inside for a quick dinner because the best part of the day was yet to come.

With water pails and hoses in reach, we took matches in hand and lit the leaf pile. The flames soon rose up to meet the stars in the dark evening sky. We danced in the cool shadows, then emerged to warm ourselves near the fire. As the last leaves flared and burned out, we slowly walked back to the house. We smelled of smoke and had crumbled leaves in our hair, but for us, it was another perfect autumn.

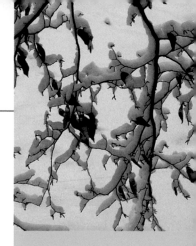

CHAPTER 4

Blow Into Winter

On cold winter nights, you may snuggle up in front of the fire, but on crisp, sunny days, we love to pile on the warm clothes and head outside to enjoy the season. Any visitors who come ill-prepared, beware! We take great joy in decking them out in old snowmobile suits and blaze-orange hunting gear. We find what we need in the cap and mitten box and we're all set for outdoor fun.

To keep warm, there's a lot of action — sledding down the hill, gliding across the ice or taking a header off the snow board. Suddenly, it all takes a turn for the worse as snow starts to fly. First one lobbing snowball falls, then another and another. Soon, it is a free-for-all with snow flying in all directions. Amid shouting and laughter, bodies tumble into the snow.

Finally, with wet faces and soggy mittens, we drag our snow-covered bodies back to the house. Glowing, but exhausted, we drop our boots by the door. Soon, there is wet clothing hanging from every available surface. The crisp and frosty air is exchanged for the rich aroma of spicy cakes, which we eagerly sample as we thaw our fingers around warm mugs of our favorite hot drinks.

SNOWBALL FIGHT BED QUILT
80" X 94"

Surround yourself with all the excitement of the day as you fall asleep under the Snowball Fight quilt. Easy snowball blocks are bordered with boots all in a row and caps and mittens hung out to dry. Make one section at a time to keep the small pieces in order.

Think of your quilt as a fabric jigsaw puzzle; not hard at all, if you take the time to lay it out one piece at a time.

Materials

4½ yd. multicolored winter print (snowball blocks, outer border)* Additional yardage may be needed to match directional prints.

1½ yd. solid blue (snowball corners, pieced border background)

1½ yd. solid white (snowball blocks)

1¼ yd. small blue check (snowball corners, boots)

1⅛ yd. red stripe (inner border, boot soles, binding)

⅝ yd. red print (snowball corners, mittens, cap bands)

⅜ yd. yellow print (snowball corners, caps, mitten bands)

8½ yd. backing fabric

Other Supplies

84" x 98" cotton batting (queen-size quilt batting)

Basic sewing tools and supplies

TIP

For easier identification, pin like pieces together and label as you cut. Group pieces for snowballs, blocks, boots, mittens and caps.

Cut

Note: WOF = width of fabric.

All fabric is based on 42"

- **Non-directional Multicolored Winter Print**

  Outer Borders

  2 lengthwise strips, 5½" x 84½"

  2 lengthwise strips, 5½" x 80½"

  Half Blocks

  7 strips, 3" x WOF

    Crosscut into

      32 rectangles, 3" x 7½"

  Corner Blocks

  4 squares, 3" x 3"

- ***Directional Multicolored Winter Print**

  Side Outer Borders

  2 lengthwise strips, 5½" x 84½"

  Top and Bottom Outer Borders

  4 strips, 5½" x WOF (Piece into 2 borders, 5½" x 80½")

  Half Blocks

  3 strips, 3" x WOF

    Crosscut into

      14 horizontal rectangles, 3" x 7½"

  3 lengthwise strips, 3" x 46"

    Crosscut into

      18 vertical rectangles, 3½" x 7½"

  Corner Blocks

  4 squares, 3" x 3"

- ***Remaining Multicolored Winter Print**

  Snowball blocks

  9 squares, 7½" x 7½"

  Snowball corners

  4 squares, 2½" x 2½"

- ***Solid Blue**

  Snowball corners

  10 strips, 2½" x WOF

    Crosscut into

      156 squares, 2½" x 2½"

  Boot A

  2 strips, 4¼" x WOF

    Crosscut into

      16 rectangles, 4" x 4¼"

  Boot B

  1 strip, 3¾" x WOF

    Crosscut into

      16 rectangles, 1" x 3¾"

  Boot C

  Use the remainder of the Boot B strip, 48 squares, 1" x 1"

  Mitten A

  3 strips, 1½" x WOF

    Crosscut into

      16 rectangles, 1½" x 6¾"

  Mitten B

  1 strip, 1½" x WOF

    Crosscut into

      8 rectangles, 1½" x 3¼"

Mitten C
1 strip, 1¼" x WOF
  Crosscut into
  8 rectangles, 1¼" x 2"
Mitten D
1 strip, 1¼" x WOF
  Crosscut into
  8 rectangles, 1¼" x 3"
Mitten E
1 strip, 1½" x WOF
  Crosscut into
  24 squares, 1½" x 1½"
Cap A
5 strips, 2" x WOF
  Crosscut into
  24 rectangles, 2" x 7½"
Cap B
1 strip, 2¾" x WOF
  Crosscut into
  24 rectangles, 1¾" x 2¾"
Cap C
1 strip, 2¼" x WOF
  Crosscut into
  24 rectangles, 1" x 2¼"
Cap D
2 strips, 2" x WOF
  Crosscut into
  24 squares, 2" x 2"

• *Solid White
  Snowball blocks
  6 strips, 7½" x WOF
    Crosscut into
    28 squares, 7½" x 7½"

• *Small Blue Check
  Snowball corners
  8 strips, 2½" x WOF
    Crosscut into
    128 squares, 2½" x 2½"
  Boot D
  2 strips, 4¼" x WOF
    Crosscut into
    16 rectangles, 4" x 4¼"
  Boot E
  4 strips, 3¼" x WOF
    Crosscut into
    16 rectangles, 3¼" x 7"

• *Red Stripe
  Borders
  8 strips, 1½" x WOF
    Piece into 2 side borders,1½" x 68½"
    Piece into a top and a bottom
    border, 1½" x 56½"
  Boot F
  4 strips, 1" x WOF
    Crosscut into
    16 rectangles, 1" x 7"
  Binding
  8 strips, 2" x WOF

DIRECTIONAL PRINTS

*For directional prints, check color diagram and lay out blocks to determine color placement for corners.

- *Red Print
  Snowball corners
  2 strips, 2½" x WOF
    Crosscut into
    32 squares, 2½" x 2½"
  Mitten F
  1 strip, 6¾" x WOF
    Crosscut into
    8 rectangles, 4½" x 6¾"
  Mitten G
  1 strip, 1½" x WOF
    Crosscut into
    8 rectangles, 1½" x 4"
  Cap F
  2 strips, 2¼" x WOF
    Crosscut into
    12 rectangles, 2¼" x 6½"

- *Yellow Print
  Snowball corners
  1 strip, 2½" x WOF
    Crosscut into
    16 rectangles, 2½" x 2½"
  Mitten H
  1 strip, 1¼" x WOF
    Crosscut into
    8 rectangles, 1¼" x 3½"
  Cap E
  2 strips, 2¾" x WOF
    Crosscut into
    12 rectangles, 2¾" x 6"

Construct

Snowball Blocks

(Make 39 multicolored winter print blocks. Make 28 white blocks.)
Draw a diagonal line on the back of all 2½" square snowball corners.
With the right sides together, place these marked squares on the cor-
ners of the 7½" square snowball blocks as shown.

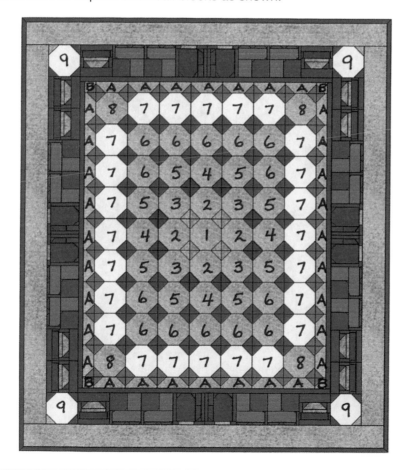

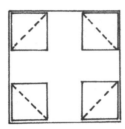

1. **Block 1:** Place a yellow print square on each of the four corners of one multicolored winter print block. Stitch on the lines.

2. **Block 2:** Place a yellow print square on two adjacent corners of four multicolored winter print blocks. Place a red print square on the two remaining corners. Stitch on the lines.

3. **Block 3:** Place a yellow print square on one corner of four multicolored winter print blocks. Place a solid blue square on the opposite corner. Place red print squares on the two remaining corners. Stitch on the lines.

4. **Block 4:** Place a red print square on two adjacent corners of four multicolored winter print blocks. Place a solid blue square on the two remaining corners. Stitch on the lines.

5. **Block 5:** Place a red print square on one corner of eight multicolored winter print blocks. Place a solid blue square on the three remaining corners. Stitch on the lines.

6. **Block 6:** Place a solid blue square on each of the four corners of 14 multicolored winter print blocks. Stitch on the lines.

7. **Block 7:** Place a solid blue square on two adjacent corners of 24 white blocks. Place a blue check square on the two remaining corners. Stitch on the line.

8. **Block 8:** Place a solid blue square on one corner of four multicolored winter print blocks. Place a blue check square on the three remaining corners. Stitch on the lines.

9. **Block 9:** Place a solid blue square on three corners of four white blocks. Place a multicolored winter print square on the fourth corner. Stitch on the line.

10. Press the stitched squares toward the corners forming snowball blocks. Trim the excess seam allowance from the corners.

Half Blocks

(Make 32 multicolored half blocks and 4 multicolored corners.)

1. **Block A:** Place a blue check square on two adjacent corners of the 32 multicolored winter print 3" x 7½" rectangles. Place squares as shown, and stitch on the lines. Press squares toward corners. Trim seam allowance.

2. **Block B:** Place a blue check square on one corner of the four 3" multicolored winter print squares. Stitch on the line. Press the stitched squares toward the corners. Trim the excess seam allowance.

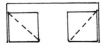 

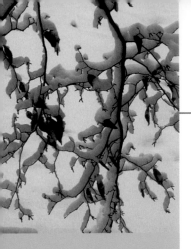

Note: Lay out all parts of the boot in proper position before constructing.

Boot Block

(Make 8 left blocks and 8 right blocks.)

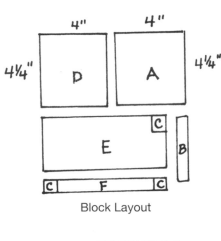

Block Layout

1. **Upper boot:** With right sides together, stitch Boot D (blue check rectangles) to Boot A (solid blue rectangles). Stitch on the 4¼" side. Press.

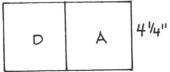

2. **Boot:** With right sides together, diagonally stitch Boot C (blue square) to the upper left corner of eight Boot E (blue check rectangles). Stitch Boot C to the upper right corner on eight of Boot E. Press toward the corners.

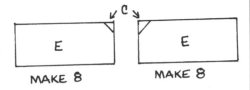

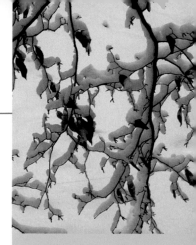

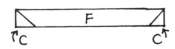

3. **Sole:** With right sides together, stitch Boot C (blue squares) to the two corners of Boot F (red stripe). Stitch diagonally as shown. Press toward corners.

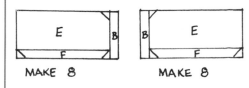

MAKE 8   MAKE 8

4. Attach the sole to the bottom of the boot. Press. Add Boot B (blue rectangle) to the tip end of the boot as shown. Press. Make eight left-facing units and eight right-facing units.

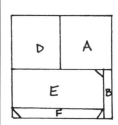

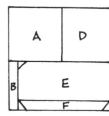

5. Attach the upper boot, making eight left boots and eight right boots.

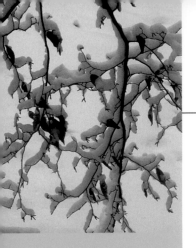

Note: Lay out all parts of the mitten in proper position before constructing.

Mitten Block

(Make 4 left blocks and 4 right blocks.)

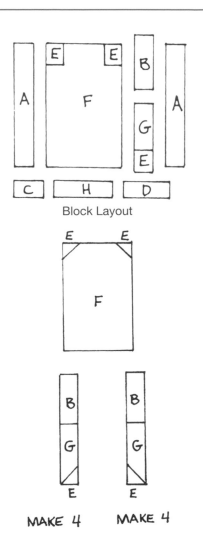

Block Layout

1. **Mitten hand:** With right sides together, diagonally stitch Mitten E (blue squares) to the two upper corners of Mitten F (red print rectangle). Press toward the corners.

2. **Mitten thumb:** Diagonally stitch Mitten E (blue square) to the corner of Mitten G (red print rectangle). Stitch four and stitch four reversed as shown. Stitch Mitten B (blue rectangle) to Mitten G.

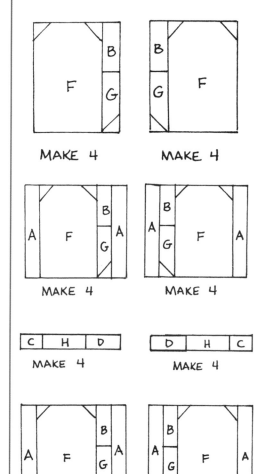

MAKE 4   MAKE 4

MAKE 4   MAKE 4

MAKE 4   MAKE 4

3. Attach B/G unit to Mitten F, making four left and four right mittens.

4. Stitch Mitten A (blue rectangles) to both sides of mitten.

5. **Mitten Band:** Stitch Mitten C (blue rectangle) to the left ends of four Mitten H (yellow rectangle). Stitch Mitten D (blue rectangle) to the right ends of four Mitten H. Make four reversed.

6. Attach the mitten bands, centering the band on the mitten.

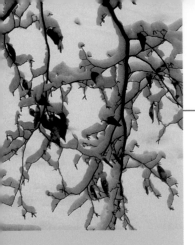

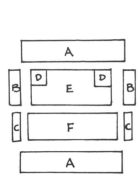

Block Layout

Cap Block
(Make 12 blocks)

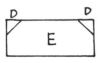

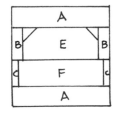

1. **Cap:** With right sides together, diagonally stitch Cap D (blue squares) to the two upper corners of Cap E (yellow print rectangle). Stitch Cap B (blue rectangles) to two ends of Cap E.

2. **Cap Band:** Stitch Cap C (blue rectangles) to two ends of Cap F (red print rectangle).

3. Attach band to cap. Stitch Mitten A (blue rectangles) to top and bottom of cap unit.

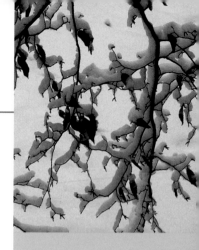

Assemble

1. Follow the illustration for colored corner placement and lay out the snowball blocks and the half blocks.*Check placement of directional prints. Stitch into rows. Stitch the rows together forming the center of the quilt top. The four remaining white snowball blocks are used in the pieced border.

2. Attach the two red stripe 68½" side borders to the quilt top. Attach the two red stripe 56½" top and bottom borders.

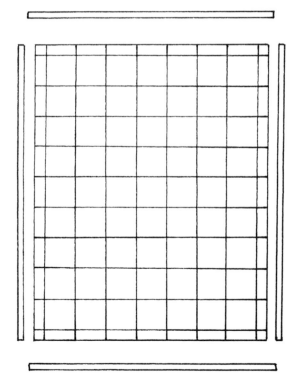

3. Assemble two pieced side borders, consisting of two cap blocks, two left boots, one left mitten, one right mitten, two right boots and ending with two cap blocks. Attach to the sides of the quilt top.

MAKE 2

4. Assemble two pieced borders for the top and bottom of the quilt, consisting of a white snowball block, one cap block, two left boots, one left mitten, one right mitten, two right boots, one cap block and ending with a white snowball block. Place the print corner of the snowball block on the lower outside corner. Attach the top and bottom pieced borders.

MAKE 2

5. Stitch the multicolored winter print, 84½"
   side borders to the quilt top. *Check placement of directional prints. Stitch the 80½"
   top and bottom borders to the quilt top.
   *Check placement of directional prints.

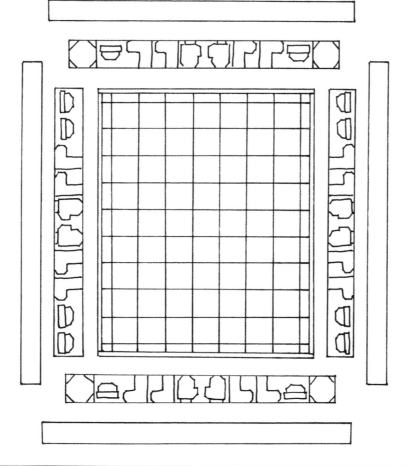

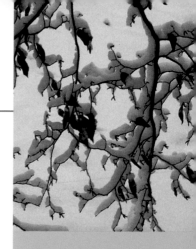

Quilt and Bind

1. Layer the quilt top, batting and backing for quilting. Baste layers together.

2. Follow the suggested quilting choices or design your own quilting motifs.

3. Stitch the binding to the quilt. Trim the batting and backing. Turn the binding to the quilt back and hand stitch. Refer to The Basics for additional instruction.

4. Add a label.

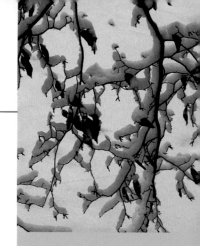

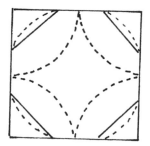
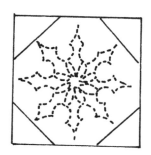
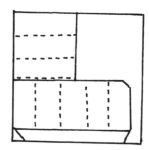

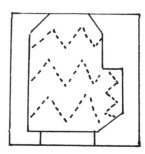
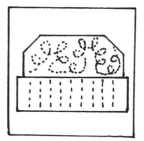

Quilting Ideas

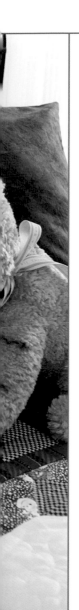

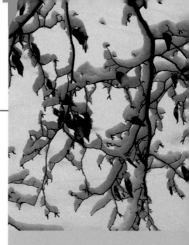

SNOWBALL PILLOWCASES
MAKES 2 STANDARD PILLOWCASES MEASURING 19½" X 30"

Finish dressing the bed with matching pillowcases. After all the activity of the day, we can't wait to lay our heads down.

Materials

1⅓ yd. solid blue (body, snowball blocks)

⅝ yd. multicolored winter print (band, snowball blocks)

⅓ yd. solid white (snowball blocks)

⅓ yd. red stripe (band trim)

½ yd. white muslin (band lining)

Basic sewing tools and supplies

Cut

- **Solid Blue:**

  2 rectangles, 22½" x 39½" (pillowcase body)

  1 strip, 1½" wide x width of fabric. Crosscut into
  24 squares, 1½" x 1½" (snowball corners)

- **Multicolored Winter Print:**

  2 strips, 5½" x 39½" (band)
  *For directional prints,
  cut 4 vertical strips, 5½" x 20"
  Piece to make two bands.

  1 strip, 1½" wide x width of fabric. Crosscut into
  24 squares, 1½" x 1½" (snowball corners)

- **Solid White**

  2 strips, 3¾"wide x width of fabric. Cross cut into
  12 squares, 3¾" x 3¾" (snowball blocks)

- **Red Stripe**

  2 rectangles, 4" x 39½" (band trim)

- **White Muslin**

  2 rectangles, 6" x 39½" (band lining)

Construct

1. Draw a line on the back of all of the 1½" snowball corners. With the right sides together, place two solid blue squares on two adjacent corners of the white snowball blocks. Place two print squares on the two remaining two adjacent corners. Stitch on the lines.

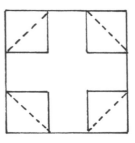

2. Press the stitched squares toward the corners, forming a snowball block. Trim the excess seam allowance from the corners.

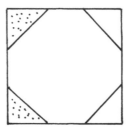

3. Make two bands of 12 snowball blocks. Stitch the blocks together with all of the solid blue corners on one edge of the band and all of the print corners on the other edge of the band. Press.

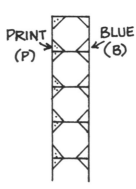

PRINT (P)   BLUE (B)

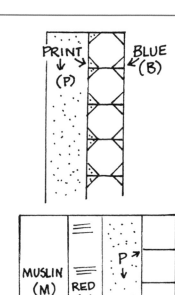

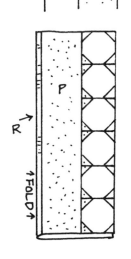

4. Stitch the snowball band to the 5½" print band, making sure the print corners are touching the print band. Press the seam allowances toward the print band.

5. Add the 4" red stripe band to the print band. Press the seam allowances toward the red stripe band.

6. Add the white muslin band to the red stripe band. Press toward the muslin.

7. Form a fold line by pressing the pillowcase border in half lengthwise revealing ¼" of the red stripe band on the edge of the print band. This will be the edge of the pillowcase when you are finished.

For directional prints, make one left and one right pillowcase.

8. Unfold, place the right sides together and stitch into a tube by joining the ends of the bands.

9. Refold on your original fold line, wrong sides together, and baste or pin raw edges together. Set aside.

10. With wrong sides together, press the solid blue body in half to measure 19¾" x 22½".

11. With right sides together, stitch two adjacent sides of the pillowcase body together. Leave open one edge adjacent to the folded edge. Serge or zigzag seams to prevent raveling. Turn pillowcase right side out.

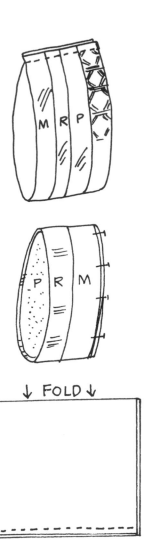

↓ FOLD ↓

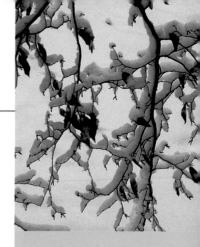

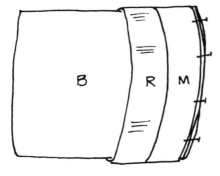

B   R   M

12. With the snowball blocks turned to the inside of the band, slide the folded band over the pillowcase. Align raw edges and pin. Match seams and pressed fold line of the pillowcase to the corresponding snowball block seams.

13. Stitch band to the pillowcase. Serge or zigzag seams. Turn band to right side and press pillowcase.

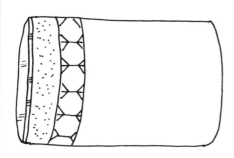

THROW SNOWBALL PILLOWS
FINISHED SIZE: 12" X 12" PILLOWS. SET OF THREE, INCLUDING ONE CAP, ONE MITTEN AND ONE BOOT PILLOW

At our house, it doesn't matter if we call them "Throw Snowball Pillows" or "Snowball Throw Pillows", there still will be pillows flying through the air. Of course, they look great on our beds, but they are more fun on the fly. Make practice blocks before making your Snowball Fight Bed Quilt. Stitch the practice blocks into small pillows to decorate the bed (or wherever they may land!) Quilted or not quilted, your choice.

Materials

½ yd. solid blue (background, inner border)

⅜ yd. small blue check (boot, outer border, pillow back)

⅜ yd. yellow print (cap, mitten band, outer border, pillow back)

⅜ yd. red print (mitten, cap band, outer border, pillow back)

1" x 7" red stripe (boot sole)

3 pillow forms, 12" x12"

3 squares 14" x 14" cotton batting (optional)

3 squares 14" x 14" muslin for quilt backing (optional)

Basic sewing tools and supplies

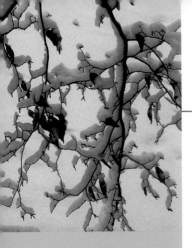

Cut

- **Solid Blue**

  6 rectangles, 9½" x 1½" (inner border)

  6 rectangles, 7½" 1½" (inner border)

  2 rectangles, 7½" x 2" (Cap A)

  2 rectangles, 2¾" x 1¼" (Cap B)

  2 rectangles, 2¼" x 1" (Cap C)

  2 squares, 2" x 2" (Cap D)

  2 rectangles, 6¾" x 1½" (Mitten A)

  1 rectangle, 3¼" x 1½" (Mitten B)

  1 rectangle, 2" x 1¼" (Mitten C)

  1 rectangle, 3" x 1¼" (Mitten D)

  3 squares, 1½" x 1½" (Mitten E)

  1 rectangle, 4" x 4¼" (Boot A)

  1 rectangle, 3¾" x 1" (Boot B)

  3 squares, 1" x 1" (Boot C)

- **Small Blue Check**

  1square, 12½" x 12½" (Boot pillow back)

  2 rectangles, 12½" x 2" (Boot outer border)

  2 rectangles, 9½" x 2" (Boot outer border)

  1 rectangle, 4¼" x 4" (Boot D)

  1 rectangle, 7" x 3¼" (Boot E)

- **Yellow Print**

  1 square, 12½" x 12½" (Cap pillow back)

  2 rectangles, 12½" x 2" (Cap outer border)

  2 rectangles, 9½" x 2" (Cap outer border)

  1 rectangle, 6" x 2¾" (Cap E)

  1 rectangle, 3½" x 1¼" (Mitten H)

- **Red Print**

  1 square 12½" x 12½" (Mitten pillow back)

  2 rectangles, 12½" x 2" (Mitten outer border)

  2 rectangles, 9½" x 2" (Mitten outer border)

  1 rectangle, 6½" x 2¼" (Cap F)

  1 rectangle, 6¾" x 4½" (Mitten F)

  1 rectangle, 4" x 1½" (Mitten G)

- **Red Stripe**

  1 rectangle, 7" x 1" (Boot F)

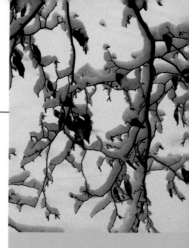

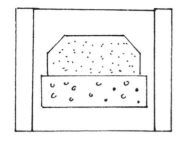

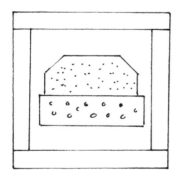

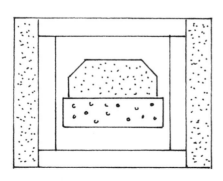

Construct

1. Following the instructions listed in the Snowball Fight Bed Quilt on page 94, construct one cap block, one mitten block, and one boot block.

2. Stitch the 7½" x 1½" solid blue inner border rectangles to the sides of the blocks. Press away from the center. (Cap block is shown, repeat for mitten block and boot block.)

3. Stitch the 9½" x 1½" solid blue inner border rectangles to the top and bottom of the block. Press away from the center.

4. Stitch the 9½" x 2" outer borders to the sides of the corresponding blocks. Press away from the center.

5. Stitch the 12½" x 2" outer borders to the top and bottom of the blocks. Press away from the center.

6. Optional Quilting: Layer top, batting and muslin quilt backing. Quilt and trim even with the pillow top.

7. With right sides together, stitch the pillow top to the pillow back. Leave an 8" opening on one side for turning. Round corners slightly as shown.

8. Turn pillow right side out and insert a pillow form.

9. Neatly stitch the opening closed

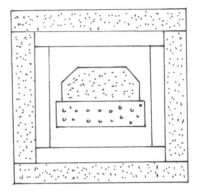

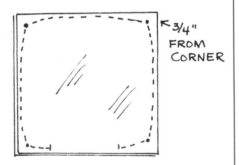

3/4" FROM CORNER

APPLE DIP

We love apples at our house and serve them often. Try sliced apples with this creamy dip for an extra special treat.

Ingredients

8 ounces crushed pineapple
1 tablespoon flour
½ cup sugar
2 tablespoons cider vinegar

1 egg, beaten
6 ounces lemon-flavored custard-style yogurt
¼ tsp ground nutmeg

1. Mix pineapple, flour, sugar, vinegar, and egg in a 2 quart pan.

2. Stirring constantly, cook over med/low heat until mixture starts to bubble. Boil one minute.

3. Remove from heat. When cool, add yogurt and nutmeg. Refrigerate.

4. Serve with fresh apple slices. Makes 1½ cups.

Nutmeg

Nutmeg was first grown in the Spice Islands that Marco Polo journeyed so far to find. In Europe, it was scarce and costly and reserved for only special uses such as holiday baking. In addition to baked foods, it is an ingredient in meatballs, eggnog, donuts, and used to enhance the flavor of many fruits.

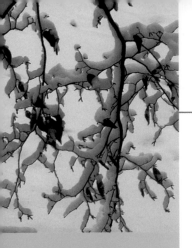

AUNT LU'S CHEWY COOKIES

As a young girl, I remember staying over night at my aunt's house and sleeping under a feather tick that seemed at least two feet thick. I munched on these yummy cookies as I giggled at my aunt's silly stories. Later, they became a favorite of my children as well. They are a perfect snack teamed with hot cider or cocoa.

Ingredients

⅞ cup shortening
1½ cup sugar
2 eggs
½ cup molasses
3 cups sifted flour

1½ teaspoons baking soda
½ teaspoon salt
1 cup shredded coconut
1 cup chopped walnuts

1. Preheat the oven to 375 degrees.

2. Cream the shortening and sugar by mixing until soft and creamy.

3. Beat in the eggs and molasses.

4. Sift together the flour, baking soda, and salt. Gradually add to the creamed mixture, mixing well.

5. Blend in the coconut and chopped nuts.

6. Drop by heaping teaspoons 2" apart unto lightly greased cookie sheets.

7. Bake for 8 to10 minutes.

With fond memories of my aunt Luella.

GUMDROP CAKE

Treasured recipes, such as this gumdrop cake, have been enjoyed and passed down by family and friends for generations. We know the "keepers" of this recipe have been making it for almost one hundred years.

Ingredients

1 cup shortening
2 cups sugar
2 eggs
4 cups flour
1 teaspoon salt
1 teaspoon baking soda
1 teaspoon cinnamon

1 teaspoon cloves
1 teaspoon nutmeg
1 teaspoon ground ginger
1½ cups applesauce
1½ cups raisins
1 cup chopped nuts
1 pound gum drops

1. Preheat the oven to 325 degrees.

2. Cream the shortening and sugar; add the eggs one at a time.

3. Sift together the flour, salt, baking soda and spices. Add to the softening mixture alternating with the applesauce.

4. Fold in the raisins, nuts, and gum drops.

5. Divide the batter between three well greased loaf pans.

6. Bake for 1 hour.

7. Remove from pans and cool before cutting.

Lil Chase
Phillips, Wis.

Ginger

Unlike most other spices, ginger is the root of the plant. It is used fresh, dried, ground, and candied. Ginger was historically used for treatment of toothaches, stomach disorders and as an antidote for the sorrows of love.

Lining Pans

Line the pans for easy loaf removal after baking. Cut a sheet of waxed paper wide enough to fit the sides and bottom of your loaf pan. Grease the ends, sides and bottom of the pan. Place the waxed paper in the pan; it will stick nicely to the greased sides. Fill with batter and bake. To remove, use a knife blade to loosen the ends and then lift or tip the loaf out.

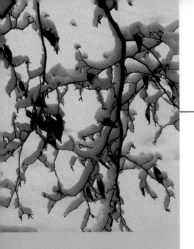

BING CHERRY SALAD

Fruit salads are a hit in every season. This brightly-colored salad filled with favorites like cream cheese, Bing cherries, and pineapple, will be a tempting side dish to perk up any meal.

Ingredients

1 package cream cheese, 8 ounces (softened)

1 cup dairy sour cream

¼ cup sugar

2 cups miniature marshmallows

1½ cup pitted Bing cherries (or 16 ounce can, drained)

1 cup crushed pineapple, drained

Red food coloring (optional)

1. Beat the cream cheese until smooth.

2. Add the sour cream and sugar. Mix well. Add food coloring, if desired.

3. Fold in marshmallows, Bing cherries and pineapple.

4. Refrigerate. (The salad may also be frozen.)

My Waldorf Salad

Back in 1946 when I was twelve years old and learning to cook, my mother asked if I would make the Waldorf salad, a family tradition, for our Christmas gathering. I was very pleased to be part of the Christmas dinner preparations. I made the salad and proudly put it on the table with all the other food. As we started to eat, my older brother, Erv, spit out the Waldorf salad and asked who made it. With tearful eyes, I confessed that I had. What I had done was put cough medicine in the salad's whipped cream instead of vanilla. The two bottles sat on the shelf next to each other. As you now know, I grabbed the wrong one. I still make that salad, but I am very careful about the vanilla. This story is still told at our family gatherings, and I have been teased about this little mistake for 60 years.

Virginia Walters
Oconomowoc, Wis.

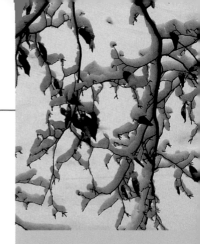

A BIRTHDAY TO REMEMBER

Birthdays are a time to gather family together, and there are some that turn out to be more memorable than others.

We invited the whole family for my young daughter's winter birthday. My brother and his family came a day before the party only to find the birthday girl down with a cold and the kitchen in total chaos because the plumbing had backed up. Soon, all the pipes in the kitchen and the basement were pulled apart, and my sister-in-law and I had to unload the dirty dishwasher and try to wash dishes in the laundry tub.

Getting hungry, we put our oven-fried chicken in to bake at 425 degrees. Suddenly, there was smoke billowing out of the oven. In all the excitement, no one remembered the baked beans had leaked over earlier in the day. With fans going and all the house doors opened, we turned around to find our little birthday girl shivering as she watched out the open front door. "Mommy, I'm waiting for the fire trucks to come!"

Jan Patlyek
Bartlett, Ill.

CHAPTER 5

The Basics

Tools and Supplies

A quilter's number one tool is the sewing machine. There are wonderful machines on the market with many different options. Specialty feet are designed to make sewing easier and more accurate. Whether you are using the newest model or a trusty old friend, keep your machine in good working order with regular maintenance. Use a new needle with each new project. Be prepared with a supply of extra universal needles as well as specific needles for quilting, or for sewing with metallic and embroidery threads.

Since good pressing can make such a difference, you will need an iron and a firm ironing surface. Spray starch can be helpful when you are working with soft or stretchy fabrics. An applique pressing sheet will help protect your iron from stray pieces of fusible web.

Rotary cutting tools, including a cutter, mat and ruler, make cutting fast and accurate. A pair of sharp dressmaker scissors is a must for all sewing projects and small thread-clipping scissors are handy at the sewing machine. Other helpful sewing supplies include a seam ripper, quilting pins, marking tools and specialty rulers. If you choose to machine quilt your own projects, you may wish to invest in tools and supplies to make the job easier. There are special sewing feet for your machine, quilting gloves, stencils and marking tools specifically for machine quilting.

Fabric

When you invest your talent and a considerable amount of your time in making a quilt, it is sensible to choose the best quality fabrics. Cotton fabrics work very well for quilting. They are easy to work with, press sharply, and can be eased into seams with less difficulty than fabric blends. Check out your local quilt shop for the latest collections of high-quality cotton fabrics.

Prepare your fabrics for quilting by pre-washing them. Occasionally, a fabric will bleed or fade and it is better to know this before you sew the fabric into your quilt. (Yes, this is the voice of experience speaking!)

For applique projects, you need a paper-backed fusible web. I have had good results with Steam-A-Seam and Lite Steam-A-Seam. Make a test sample, taking care to follow the manufacturer's suggestions for temperature settings on your iron, as some products have lower melting points than others.

When quilting your project, cotton and cotton-blend battings work well because they have rougher surface textures and don't shift as you stitch. This is especially important for machine quilting. I find Hobbs Heirloom Premium Cotton Batting, 80% cotton/20% polyester, a good choice for both hand and machine quilting.

Binding the Quilt:

A narrow binding gives a nice, crisp edge to your finished quilt. Although binding strips may be cut on the bias, cutting on the straight grain of the fabric also works well for straight edge quilts.

1. **Cutting:** Cut the binding strips 2" wide across the width (or length) of the fabric. Cut enough strips to exceed the circumference of the quilt.

2. **Piecing strips:** The strips can be easily joined while seated at your sewing machine. Overlap the ends of two strips, both right side up, and cut at an angle. This does not have to be a precise 45-degree angle, as you are cutting through both strips at the same time and you will cut the same angle on both strips.

3. Align the strips at the ¼" seam allowance and stitch a diagonal seam. By piecing diagonally, you will spread the bulk of the seam allowance so it won't be concentrated at one spot.

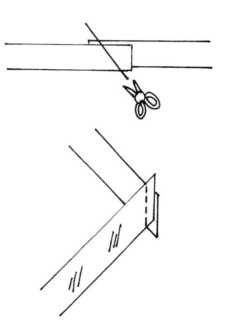

QUILT
TOP

4. Piece the binding together as needed. The length of your binding should be approximately 6" longer than your quilt circumference. Press the seam allowances open.

5. Press the binding in half lengthwise, wrong sides together, to make a 1" strip.

6. **Adding Binding to the Quilt:** Leaving a 3" tail of binding, start stitching the binding along one side of the quilt. Match the raw edges of the binding to the edge of the quilt top and stitch a ¼" seam.

7. Stop stitching ¼" before the corner of the quilt. With the needle down, pivot the quilt to align with the second side of the quilt. Backstitch to the edge of the quilt top, approximately four stitches.

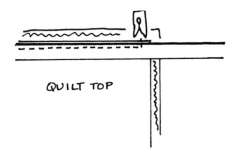

8. With the needle down, raise the foot and fold the binding back to the needle and even with the second edge of the quilt. (A stiletto or your seam ripper will be helpful for this task.) Under the fold, a 45-degree miter will form. Continue stitching along the second side of the quilt.

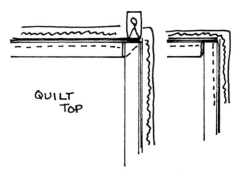

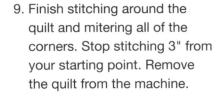

9. Finish stitching around the quilt and mitering all of the corners. Stop stitching 3" from your starting point. Remove the quilt from the machine.

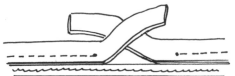

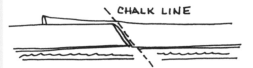

CHALK LINE

10. **Joining the Ends:** Leaving the binding folded, trim the starting end on a diagonal. Lay this end over the finished end and draw a pencil or chalk line at the overlap.

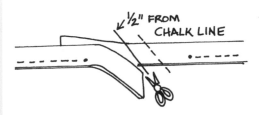

½" FROM CHALK LINE

11. Trim binding ½" longer than this drawn line.

12. Align the folded binding ends at the ¼" seam line and stitch. Backstitch at the folded edge. Press open the seam allowance.

13. The binding should now fit exactly to the quilt edge. Stitch in place, overlapping the previous seams to secure the stitching.

14. **Finishing the binding:** Trim the backing and batting even with the quilt top. Add a rod pocket to the top of your quilt, if desired. Fold the binding to the quilt back.

15. Hand stitch the binding to the quilt back. Form a folded miter at the corners. Trim or tuck under the seam allowance tail at the point where the binding was joined.

QUILT BACK

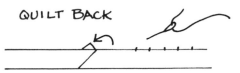

Adding a Rod Pocket

If you plan to hang your quilt, you can add a rod pocket to the top of the back. Although a rod pocket can be hand stitched to the back after the quilt is finished, it is quicker to add it before the binding is completed.

1. Cut a strip of fabric 8½" wide by 2" less than the width of the quilt. Finish the ends of the rod pocket by folding the ends ½" to the wrong side of the fabric, and fusing them in place with a narrow strip of fusible web. Press the rod pocket in half lengthwise, wrong sides together.

2. Center the rod pocket strip on the back of the quilt with the raw edges even with the top of the quilt. Stitch a ¼" seam to secure the rod pocket to the back of the quilt. You will be stitching on the same seam line that attached the binding to the front of the quilt.

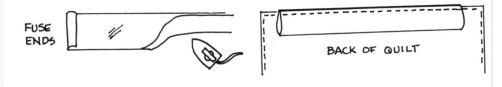

FUSE ENDS

BACK OF QUILT

3. Fold the binding to the back of the quilt, and hand stitch the bottom of the rod pocket to the back of the quilt. Be careful to keep the stitches from coming through to the right side of the quilt.

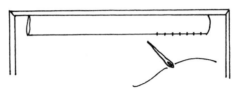

Adding a Label

Adding a label is the perfect finishing touch for your project. You can draw your own label, choose a preprinted one, or use a computer program to create and print a label on printable fabric sheets. Be sure to include your name as the quiltmaker and the year the quilt was finished. If this is a special gift, include the name of the recipient and any history of the quilt or the special occasion commemorated. Don't forget care instructions so your quilt can be enjoyed for many years to come.

Contributors and Resources

American and Efird, Inc.
www.amefird.com
Threads and yarns
P.O. Box 507
Mt. Holly, NC 28120
(800) 847-3235

Michael Miller Fabrics, LLC
www.michaelmillerfabrics.com
Fabrics for quilting, sewing and crafts
118 W. 22nd St., 5th Floor
New York, NY 10011
(212) 704-0774

Hobbs Bonded Fibers
www.hobbsbondedfibers.com
Battings, pillow inserts, and fiberfill
P.O. Box 2521
Waco, TX 76702-2521
(800) 433-3357

Prym Consumer, USA
www.dritz.com
Sewing, quilting, cutting and craft-related tools and notions
P.O. Box 5028
Spartanburg, SC 29304
(800) 845-4948

Robert Kaufman Co., Inc.
www.robertkaufman.com
Fabric supplier and converter of
quilting fabrics and textiles for
manufacturers
129 W. 132nd St.
Los Angeles, CA 90061
(800) 877-2066

The Warm Co.
www.warmcompany.com
Batting and fusible products
954 E. Union St.
Seattle, WA 98122
(800) 234-9276

Superior Threads
www.superiorthreads.com
Quality threads for longarm and home
machines
P.O. Box 1672
St. George, Utah 84771
(800) 499-1777

ADDITIONAL RESOURCES

Annie's Attic
www.anniesattic.com
1 Annie Lane
Big Sandy, TX 75755
(800) 582-6643

Clotilde, LLC
www.clotilde.com
P.O. Box 7500
Big Sandy, TX 75755-7500
(800) 772-2891

Connecting Threads
www.ConnectingThreads.com
P.O. Box 870760
Vancouver, WA 98687-7760
(800) 574-6454

Herrschners, Inc.
www.herrschners.com
2800 Hoover Road
Stevens Point, WI 54492-0001
(800) 441-0838

Home-Sew Inc.
www.homesew.com
P.O. Box 4099
Bethlehem, PA 18018-0099
(800) 344-4739

Keepsake Quilting
www.keepsakequilting.com
Route 25
P.O. Box 1618
Center Harbor, NH 03226-1618
(800) 438-5464

Nancy's Notions
www.nancysnotions.com
333 Beichl Ave.
P.O. Box 683
Beaver Dam, WI 53916-0683
(800) 833-0690

Krause Publications
www.krausebooks.com
(800) 258-0929

Brother International Corp.
www.brothersews.com
(800) 422-7684

Husqvarna/Viking
www.husqvarnaviking.com
(800) 358-0001

Baby Lock
www.babylock.com
(800) 422-2952

Bernina
www.berninausa.com
(800) 405-2738

Janome
www.janome.com
(800) 631-0183

Pfaff
www.pfaff.com
(800-997-3233

Singer
www.singershop.com
(800) 474-6437

About the Author

Sharon V. Rotz has been sharing her passion for quilting with students for the past 20 years. She has designed her own pattern line, By Sher, and has authored "Log Cabin Quilts with Attitude," (Krause Publications).

Her prize-winning quilts have been shown in art gallery exhibits as well as national and international quilt shows. As a textile artist, her work has been purchased by medical facilities, museums, and numerous private collectors.

A graduate of the University of Wisconsin-Stout, Sharon has worked in the ready-made clothing industry, and operated her own business creating custom clothing and furnishings.

The rural life style and the ever-changing seasons of central Wisconsin where she lives, are a constant source of inspiration.

She feels blessed to share her life with her husband, Tom, their two children and spouses, and three bubbly grandchildren in a loving circle of family and friends.

Visit Sharon online at www.bysher.net.

More Smart Stitchin' Instructions

Quilt With Confidence
by Nancy Zieman

The inspiring and encouraging tone of this book will make you feel like you've been quilting your entire life! From the nation's favorite sewing teacher comes tips and step-by-step instruction for getting started quilting, from selecting tools, to rotary cutting techniques and edge-joined seaming, you get it all!

Softcover • 8-1/4 x 10-7/8 • 144 pages
Item# Z1549 • $24.99

90-Minute Quilts
15+ Projects You Can Make in an Afternoon
by Meryl Ann Butler

Discover how easy it is to create stylish baby and large lap quilts, plus wall hangings using the quick tips, methods and 250 how-to color photos and illustrations included in this book.

Hardcover • 8 x 8 • 160 pages
250 color photos and illus.
Item# NTYMQ • $24.99

Quilts From My Garden
20 Projects With Recipes Fresh from the Garden
by Karen Snyder

Quilting and cooking, while they may not go hand-in-hand for everyone, there's something refreshing about creating items using "recipes," regardless if it's stitching or stirring. Luckily, with this book you get recipes for both, through partner projects including hot pads and Corn Relish.

Softcover • 8-1/4 x 10-7/8 • 128 pages
100+ color photos
Item# Z1320 • $19.99

Quilting
The Complete Guide
by Darlene Zimmerman

Everything you need to know to quilt is in this book. It contains more than 400 color photos and illustrations demonstrating the quilt making process.

Hardcover • 5-5/8 x 7-5/8 • 256 pages
400 color photos and illus.
Item# Z0320 • $29.99

Chameleon Quilts
Versatile Looks Using Traditional Patterns
by Margrit Hall,
Foreword by Earlene Fowler

Learn how to use new fabrics, colors and textures and the same set of 10 quilt patterns to create 19 different projects. Features more than 200 step-by-step color photos and graphics.

Softcover • 8-1/4 x 10-7/8 • 128 pages
200+ color photos
Item# Z0104 • $22.99